THINKING & LIVING SKILLS:

GENERAL SEMANTICS FOR CRITICAL THINKING

The publication of this book was
made possible by contributions from:

D. David Bourland, Jr.
Paul Dennithorne Johnston
Rachel M. Lauer
Edward MacNeal
Mary S. Morain
Charlotte Schuchardt Read
Dennis Reuter
Mitsuko Saito-Fukunaga
Gregory Guy Sawin
Charles E. Scripps
Dennis and Virginia Wile

Thinking & Living Skills:

General Semantics for Critical Thinking

Edited by

Gregory Sawin

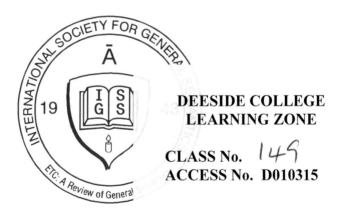

INTERNATIONAL SOCIETY FOR GENERAL SEMANTICS

CONCORD, CALIFORNIA

THINKING & LIVING SKILLS:
GENERAL SEMANTICS FOR CRITICAL THINKING
Copyright © 1995 by the International Society for General Semantics

Cover and art design: G. Sawin
Layout: P. D. Johnston

Printed in the United States of America

International Society for General Semantics
P.O. Box 728
Concord, CA 94522, USA

Library of Congress Cataloging-in-Publication Data

Thinking & living skills : general semantics for critical thinking /
edited by Gregory Sawin.
    p. cm.
  Includes bibliographical references and index.
  ISBN 0-918970-42-3 (pbk.)
  1. General semantics. 2. Critical thinking. 3. Schemas
(Psychology) 4. Schematism (Philosophy) 5. Interpersonal
communication. 6. Quality of life. I. Sawin, Gregory, 1950- .
B820.T45 1995
149'.94--dc20   95-681
                                                          CIP

CONTENTS

PART 4: CRITICAL THINKING

PART 5: CULTURES: FROM BUILDING
WALLS TO BUILDING BRIDGES

Preface

by Gregory Sawin

O N THE EVENING of January 28, 1980, my friend, Greg B. Phillips, arrived at my house for his regular weekly visit. During our conversation, he made a casual offer that triggered a chain of events destined to change my life. He merely suggested that I might like to read *The World of Null-A*, an award-winning science-fiction story about a 26th-century man trained in a special kind of "logic." (1-4)

My friend knew that for years I worried about the personally and socially destructive effects of illogical human behavior, so he showed no surprise when I asked to borrow his book. Reading that intriguing story provided me with a tantalizing taste of general semantics. I had discovered an exciting subject that could help me cultivate more powerful thinking skills than the pure logic I learned in school. General semantics seemed light-years beyond "semantics" because it offered me new ways to think, communicate, act, and react.

Immediately, I realized the relevance of it for improving my life.

When I returned the book to my friend, I felt content with my new gems of wisdom. But, to my surprise, I soon found that I could not stop thinking about them. I *had* to learn more about these fascinating ideas, so I began reading general semantics books cover to cover. For me, that first close encounter with general semantics felt like finding buried treasure.

In addition to studying these methods for better thinking and living, I started using a few of them to deal with the choices and challenges in my daily life.

In the course of a decade, applying these new ideas helped me do the following:

- Think clearly and flexibly

- Communicate accurately
- Argue less often and listen more carefully
- Understand the tricks used by some persuaders in their attempts to sell me a product, an idea, or a lottery ticket
- Distinguish between statements of fact versus statements of opinion, objective reports versus prejudiced judgments, and, in general, sense versus nonsense
- Cultivate a fine-tuned awareness of possibilities that has increased my ability to avoid accidents, especially car accidents.

Using the thinking and living skills of general semantics brings me great rewards: I have fewer unnecessary problems and bad experiences.

Now for comments on general semantics from others:

"[In a general semantics seminar*] participation ... provided me with a safe and supportive environment in which I could understand and practice the [general semantics] principles. As a result, I came away with a deeper understanding and appreciation of life as a process, rather than an event. I feel more confident in coping with life's situations and interpersonal relationships." (5)

JANE BACHMAN

"I wish every student in high school had the opportunity to take a class in general semantics.... students seem to love using what we study in class.... I enjoy hearing about how an inference led one astray, how a nonsense argument was resolved,... or how eliminating *to be* made a difference in how they perceived the world. Certainly students see the relevance of the course." (6)

RUTH McCUBBREY

---

* This 1991 summer seminar took place at Alverno College, a women's college in Milwaukee, Wisconsin. It was conducted by instructors from the Institute of General Semantics, 163 Engle St., Englewood, NJ 07631.

"I have taught general semantics concepts [in high school] since 1963 .... Student response has remained positive, even enthusiastic. I now have the children of former students in the classes." (7)

RICHARD J. DOVGIN

"As a new [high school] teacher in 1970, I wrote a semester English course called 'Introduction to Semantics'.... I used *Language in Thought and Action* as a source.... During its height, I had 300 students a year for an eight year period ....At last count, I have exposed more than 4,000 students in varying degrees to the principles of general semantics.... The feedback from past students is gratifying .... I think general semantics has touched their lives." (8)

WILLIAM DOHERTY

"While 'everyone' around us was teaching and talking about 'common sense', Korzybski [the founder of general semantics], for the first time, introduced the uncommon sense of an Einstein to everyday thinking, communicating and behaving." (9)

SANFORD I. BERMAN

Many of the following selections from *Et cetera* (1986-1993) describe the usefulness of general semantics in different situations. (10) Open the treasure chest of general semantics, behold the gems of wisdom, take as many as you want, and begin the adventure of discovering important rewards when you apply them in your life.

NOTES AND REFERENCES

1. A.E. van Vogt, *The World of Null-A*, (A.E. van Vogt, 1945; this book has been translated into nine languages); Ariel Press Edition 1989, Canal Winchester, OH; also available from the International Society for General Semantics.

2. A.E. van Vogt, *The Players of Null-A*, (1948); Ariel Press, 1989; also available from the International Society for General Semantics.

3. A.E. van Vogt, *Null-A Three*, New York, DAW Books, Inc., 1985.

4. H.L. Drake, A.E. van Vogt's General-Semantics Worlds, *General Semantics Bulletin*, no. 54 (1988-1989), Institute of General Semantics, Englewood, NJ, 73-80.

5. Jane Bachman, *Et cetera 48*, no. 4 (Winter 1991-92), 441.

6. Ruth McCubbrey (high school English and general semantics teacher), *Et cetera 45*, no. 2 (Summer 1988), 176.

7. Richard J. Dovgin, *Et cetera 49*, no. 4 (Winter 1992-93), 457.

8. William Doherty, *Et cetera 49*, no. 4 (Winter 1992-93), 456-457.

9. Sanford I. Berman (former lecturer on effective communication at the University of Chicago and Northwestern University, President of Educational Cassettes and past-president of the ISGS), *Et cetera 46*, no. 4 (Winter 1989), 356.

10. *Et cetera*, published quarterly by the International Society for General Semantics, was founded by the late S. I. Hayakawa. In 1993, we celebrated the journal's 50th Anniversary. Now, thousands of Society members in 50 countries enjoy reading *Et cetera*.

"General semantics...is something you do."

—Irving J. Lee

The Relevance of General Semantics

by Alvin Toffler

Dropping in at the 1988 International Conference on General Semantics at Yale University, Alvin Toffler was invited by program chairman William Exton to speak. These are his remarks.

I WAS HOPING to sneak in here, because I am a rank amateur at general semantics, but over the years I have had a memory of an evening with Korzybski at Columbia University years ago. And I, of course, read *Science and Sanity*.

On the way down here tonight I stopped to ask myself what I had retained. I think I can list very simply what stuck, and I can easily see how it connects with the work I have done since. Clearly, Korzybski was not my only influence —

Author of *Future Shock*, *The Third Wave*, many other books, and numerous articles, Alvin Toffler is one of the world's best-known thinkers on the dynamics of social and cultural change. (1)

all of us are bombarded by stimuli and ideas from all over the place; but I think that many of the things that I have written are at least compatible with what general semantics would hold.

Among the things that I realized that stuck, were, first, the whole idea of non-Aristotelian logic, which was a completely new idea to me, but made an awful lot of sense. Reality did not come packaged with "either-ors" — at least to me — and I think that is still a part of the way I like to analyze things. I think in terms of multiple models, rather than a single model. I think of things overlapping, blending into each other, and so on; and change, which is my preoccupation, is really a complex process.

Time-Binding

The second idea is time-binding. Time has been central to my writing because my writing has focused on the issue of change, and change is a function of time, or vice versa. In *Future Shock*, I wrote about the acceleration of change, about different cultures' perceptions of time and the different paces of life, all of them being time phenomena. And, of course, as one who is called a "futurist," I spend a lot of my time thinking about the past as well. It seems to me that one is not fully a person if one does not see oneself in a temporal perspective that reaches back through the eighty billion human beings who preceded us since our own earliest beginnings and forward in time, as it were, to the stars, which somehow symbolize the future, though what we see when we look at them is, in fact, the past.

The Map Is Not the Territory

The third idea is that the map is not the territory. It is a humbling notion for a writer because I am busy producing  maps, and that is my function in life — aside from being human. In the introduction of *Future Shock*, indeed, I wrote about cartography and the need for even primitive maps. Primitive maps are better than no maps. Nevertheless I realize deeply the difference between the map I am writing about and the reality that I can't quite get down on paper, no matter how hard I try.

I remember one experience when I was a journalist in Washington, covering a Senate hearing. I went home that night to write the story. I had sat in the room for several hours listening to the speakers on disarmament statistics, ballistic missiles, and nuclear weapons, and so on, and I sat down to write the story. I had about 500 words to condense it into and knew that my story would be on page one the next day. But no matter how many times I wrote it, and how many different approaches I used, somehow I knew that I couldn't capture the full reality. That led me to think about the front page of that newspaper — or any newspaper. I knew my story would run on page one alongside nine or ten other stories by other journalists who were also writing, who were also not capturing the full reality they were reporting. Some of them may have been more intelligent than I, or some less, and some more responsible, some less. So that since then, I have regarded page one of the newspaper as a kind of fiction, a distorted map of a territory, too complex and too fast-changing to map. Nevertheless it is a fiction that we live by.

Finally, "the map is not the territory" leads me to the notion that all assumptions should be challenged. We live in a maze of what I call an "architecture of assumptions." We build assumption upon assumption upon assumption, and we wind up with abstract notions like "productivity" that become obsolete as accelerative change undermines them. The result is the idiocy of the conceptual categories used by, say, economists — categories that don't match the territory, but categories which they somehow can't give up. That takes me from categories to metaphors and names.

Future Shock

Naming is very important to an author, and titles sometimes register and sometimes don't. I have often been asked about the origins of the concepts of "future shock" and the "third wave." The process by which future shock was arrived at was basically analogy. I was interested in the phenomenon of "culture shock," and was interviewing a psychologist one day, a friend of mine, asking her about the symptoms of culture shock and what causes culture shock. As we spoke, it occurred to me in the course of that interview that if you could be disoriented by being relocated in space, that you could also be disoriented by being relocated in time, and that the rapidity of change has a similar effect on our culture and our people. The idea of future shock sprang from that analogy with culture shock, a transposition from space to time.

The Third Wave

In the case of the "third wave," there are many theories of economic and social development. Rostow wrote a book in the fifties called *The Stages of Growth* which became one of the dominant texts on the strategy of economic development in the third world. My wife and I thought the notion of stages too static and unidimensional, while the image of waves of change suggests a less mechanical and potentially multidimensional process. As you know, we use the "first wave" to mean the processes associated with agriculturalization and the agrarian era; the "second wave" to mean the processes of industrialization and the industrial era; and the "third wave" to mean the changes forming a new society today. That is the way we use the metaphor of waves. And the nice thing about it for us is that waves suggest change, motion and process. But even better, it is also possible for *multiple* waves of change to course through society simultaneously. It is also analogically interesting because when waves collide, you get conflict, you get cross-currents. For these reasons, we felt the metaphor of waves offers a powerful way to characterize periods of fundamental change in society. But again, it is just a metaphor, and so all of the questions that are raised by *Science and Sanity* are inherent or should be inherent in the work of any thinking writer or communicator. In short, the emphasis on process that Korzybski stressed is present in all the intellectual work my wife and I have done over the years.

I thank you for what you are doing. I popped in on just a whim, knowing I was just an hour away, and I thank you for letting me crash your party.

NOTE

1. See the "Notes About the Authors" section for a list of Mr. Toffler's published works.

From *Et cetera* 46, no. 3 (Fall 1989) pages 197-199.

"Every human being is an amphibian..."

"We are ... floating in the given reality of our physiology, of our intuitions and perceptions, our pains and pleasures, but projecting at the same time into the airy world of words and notions.... Living amphibiously, half in fact and half in words ... we contrive most of the time to make the worst of both worlds.... Our business as human beings is to make the best of both these worlds."

—Aldous Huxley

(From his book, *Tomorrow and Tomorrow and Tomorrow and Other Essays*, Harper & Bros., New York, 1952, pp. 1–7)

Time-Binding:
To Build a Fire

by James D. French

P ERHAPS WE KNEW about fire before we even knew we were
human. We were using fire to drive and trap animals and
to roast meat 500,000 years ago, during the Pleistocene Era.
However, exactly when or how *Homo Erectus* discovered fire
is unknown, although there are theories: A woman may have
been chipping flakes from a piece of flint, and the sparks that
flew from the blows ignited nearby leaves and twigs; then
again, there may have been a lightning strike and a forest
fire, and our man Grog took a burning branch home to light
and warm the cave.

From One Generation to the Next

Of course, the generations of humans that came after the
great discovery started out life with the knowledge of fire, a
knowledge passed to them in childhood by their parents. Because it is in the nature of human beings to pass information

from one generation to the next — to build on the achievements of past generations over time — there was no turning back to prefire days. Each generation added to the storehouse of knowledge about fire until, by the Neolithic Era, humans could produce fire at will, with such tools as the fire drill and the bow drill.

In 1669, phosphorus, a volatile, deadly poison, and the starter ingredient of modern matches, was discovered. John Walker, an Englishman, built on that discovery and produced the first practical friction match in 1827. In 1855, the safety match appeared; it could only be lighted when struck against a strip of red phosphorus. Finally, the Diamond Match Company created a safe, non-poisonous phosphorus formula in 1911 from a French patent, and the modern match came into being.

It may seem strange, but even such a simple task as striking a match is not an entirely independent act; it is the result of the efforts of countless generations over time.

Ten years after the appearance of the Diamond match, Alfred Korzybski formulated a new theory of human existence based on the interdependence of the generations. He saw, as we have seen in the history of fire, the links between the generations that are integral to the development of human culture. In the words of Abraham Lincoln:

Fishes, birds, beasts, and creeping things are not miners, but feeders and lodgers merely.   Beavers build houses; but they build them in no wise differently or better now than they did five thousand years ago. Ants and honey bees provide food for winter; but just in the same way they did when Solomon referred the sluggard to them as patterns of prudence. Man is not the only animal who labors; but he is the only one who improves his workmanship. (1)

Classes of Life

Korzybski called his theory "time-binding." (2) He said that there are three primary classes of life: plants, animals, and human beings; and each of these classes can be distinguished according to its function.

Plants take in energy from the sun and the atmosphere and convert it into chemical elements and compounds through the process of photosynthesis. The chemicals are released back to the atmosphere or stored and later converted into growth and plant tissue; and thus plants may be called the *chemical-binding* class of life.

Animals take in stored energy from plants and other animals, and from the atmosphere, and use it for mobility. Animals are the *space-binding* class of life, because unlike plants, they can voluntarily move about in terrestrial space — they can roam about over the land or in the sea in search of food (energy).

Human beings use stored chemical energy and the ability to move over the land to discover and develop knowledge and information. Human knowledge is stored in the minds of individuals and in books and other media, and is passed with the aid of language to the next generation. This process creates new sources of energy: for example, the applied knowledge of plant cultivation produces more food energy than would otherwise be available. By storing knowledge and information, the achievements of each generation are passed to the next generation, which in turn adds its own achievements and passes them on to its descendants, and so on, as in the case of fire. Thus, as a species, we have a degree of interdependence that is greater by far than that of any animal. Consider the millions of human beings who would not be alive today were it not for the medical knowledge (of vaccination, for example) discovered and passed on by bygone generations. Not only do we depend on those now living, we also depend on the countless individuals of the past; and future generations depend on us. Because we have this special ability, this unique capacity to advance through time, we are the *time-binding class of life*.

Time-Binding

Humans, as time-binders, do not differ in kind from animals, but in dimension, just as a square and a cube are the same kind of figure but different in dimension. Through our special ability to utilize the time dimension, we have achieved a level of existence unknown to that of the beasts. Of course, it is possible that animals may also have a limited capacity to bind time; but if so, then it must be at a negligible rate. It is our unique, unmatched rate that sets us apart. If all that we have gained in the course of time — art, industry, language, philosophy, religion, and science — were to be suddenly taken away from us, it would be impossible for an outside observer to distinguish between our behavior and that of the beasts. In large measure, time-binding is what makes human beings *human*.

It seems evident that Korzybski's theory has important social implications. Consider the ethical question of whether egoism comes before altruism. Egoism seems to come first for animals because, as Herbert Spencer said, "A creature must live before it can act"; but does it come first for the time-binding class of life? Korzybski said no. Human beings, because of our time-binding capacity, are not finders but *creators* of food and shelter, which is why we are able to live in such vast numbers. Thus we must act first (by utilizing our time-binding ability) in order to live. Otherwise, said Korzybski, if we were to live in complete accord with the animalistic view of humankind, time-binding production would cease and ninety percent of humankind would perish by starvation. For the human race, it's not inevitably a "dog-eat-dog world"; we have the capacity and opportunity to act otherwise.

For the society that adopts it, Korzybski's theory could provide a secure, rational foundation for ethical behavior, an ethics based on the verifiable fact of human interdependence in time and space. If taught well in the schools, the theory could transform the whole outlook of our culture. Because time-binding is fully compatible with the great religions and science, it can be the foundation of a new American ethic.

The future depends in large part both upon what we human beings *are* and in equal or greater measure upon what we *think we are*. We are the time-binding class of life. (3)

REFERENCES

1. Quoted by W.N. Polakov, *Man and His Affairs* (Baltimore, MD, Williams & Wilkins Co., 1925) 61-62.
2. C. J. Keyser, Korzybski's Concept of Man, in A. Korzybski, *Manhood of Humanity* (E.P. Dutton & Co., 1921; 2d edition 1950, Englewood, NJ, Institute of General Semantics).
3. Ibid., 314; also see 305-307.

From *Et cetera* 46, no. 3 (Fall 1989) pages 194-196.

Time-Binder

Space-Binder

Chemistry-Binder

Time-Binding

by Gregory Sawin

D URING WORLD WAR I, Alfred Korzybski volunteered for service in the army. Appalled by the suffering and destruction he witnessed during the war, he asked himself "Why?" He noted the long history of destructive human behavior, but he did not neglect the equally impressive and vast record of constructive human achievement. Technological advances led to artifacts of modern civilization such as skyscrapers, bridges, dams, aircraft, automobiles, radios, and telephones.

The Power to Create and Destroy

Korzybski wasn't sure why people destroy each other in war or how they created civilizations. To find out, he thought it important to answer the question, "What makes human beings human?" He wanted to know what was distinctive about our species. His background in engineering and science led him to seek an answer in terms of what people *do*.

He realized that humans transmit information from one generation to the next, and that a younger generation can begin where an older one left off. (1) Animals don't do this to any significant extent compared to humans. For example, from generation to generation, beaver dams don't change much. But over generations of human activity, people created and accumulated written records of their discoveries, inventions, and ideas about dams. People of later generations used libraries and attended universities and institutes to study, discuss, test, modify, and retest these ideas, all the while keeping written records of their progress. This process resulted in the building of better and better dams. Many modern dams are masterpieces of engineering, a far cry from beaver dams. So, as far as dam building was concerned, generations of humans didn't just leave it to beavers. (2)

Time-Binding

"Time-binding" is what Korzybski called this uniquely human ability to survive in the present by learning from the past to prepare for the future. Hayakawa wrote: "This network of cooperation we have created is intricate and complex, and it has been relatively effective ... all this coordination of effort necessary for the functioning of society is of necessity achieved by language or else it is not achieved at all." (3) Hayakawa also noted that "The cultural accomplishments of the ages ... come to us as *free gifts from the dead*. These gifts ... offer us not only the opportunity for a richer life than our forebears enjoyed but also the opportunity to add to the sum total of human achievement by our own contributions..." (4)

Time-binding appears to be a fundamental aspect of life in all cultures. We are time-binders — not only have we created languages to collect information and transmit it to people in the present and to people of the future, but we also teach our children to develop their time-binding skills so they can understand and profit from knowledge of older generations. *This* is what human beings *do*. The mathematical philosopher Cassius Jackson Keyser called time-binding "not an effect of civilization but ... its cause." (5)

In 1921, Korzybski's time-binding theory was published in his first book, *Manhood of Humanity*. He maintained that "All human achievements, constructive or destructive, are manmade, and so to properly evaluate them, we have to understand the mechanism of how this fundamental ... [time-binding] activity of humans works." (6) Although he had formulated some answers to his questions, an understanding of the mechanism of time-binding eluded him. His obsession to improve the quality of human life compelled him to investigate.

His time-binding theory explained something about what people do as members of a group. But it took him years of laborious research to realize which particular functions of an individual enable him or her to contribute to, and profit from, group time-binding behavior.

The approach he used in his research was derived from his scientific training; he knew that the sciences provide useful methods for problem solving. Korzybski rejected the theological and zoological definitions of a human being. He began by studying facts: he studied what people *do*. He labored for twelve years to develop his "human engineering" methodology. It explained in detail the mechanisms of time-binding, and also provided insights for more successful time-binding behavior. Later, Korzybski changed the name "human engineering" to "general semantics." (7) I believe this is what he meant when he wrote that "Humanity, civilizations, cultures, etc., are ultimately based on the constructive use of neuro-semantic and neuro-linguistic mechanisms present in every one of us." (8)

In 1933, Korzybski published his second book, *Science and Sanity*, which explained general semantics in detail. It dealt primarily with the functioning of an individual human being as a whole: the interactions among the perceptual, neurological, physiological, psychological, linguistic, and behavioral processes involved in making sense of (and in reacting to) the stream of events in everyday life.

Two Ways of Gaining Knowledge

Korzybski believed that the first step in using general semantics to minimize human problems was to become conscious of the difference between the verbal levels and the silent, nonverbal levels of human functioning. (9) His idea can be clarified by Robert Pula's definition: "In general semantics we're concerned with the relationships between symbol systems and nervous systems as expressed in behavior." (10) Basically, a person has two ways of acquiring knowledge: "first-hand information" — seeing, hearing, tasting it for oneself by using one's sense organs and nervous system; and "second-hand information" — receiving information conveyed by a language or another symbol system.

Here are a few examples of first-hand experience:

- Eating an apple to discover how it tastes.
- Meeting and talking with someone to get an idea about what that person is like.
- Feeling the pain of your toothache.

Examples of second-hand experience are the following:

- You read a description of an apple.
- A co-worker tells you about someone you haven't met.
- Someone tells you about his painful toothache.

Each of us lives in these two "worlds": the nonverbal world of direct, personal experience of happenings around us (and inside us), and the verbal world of words, and other symbols, that we use to send and receive messages about real or imagined happenings. Whatever we think we know about the world comes to us through these channels. This "knowledge" shapes our beliefs, interests, expectations, fears, and goals. It molds our attitudes about ourselves and other people. It even influences our choice of strategies for coping with life.

The Quality of Life

For Korzybski, improving the quality of human life meant providing ways for people to cultivate more skillful thinking, become more successfully adjusted to the world around them, work together more effectively and get more of what they want out of life. He wanted to provide us with methods for building a saner, more productive, and happier future. He wrote, "This new functional definition of humans as time-binders ... explains ... how we humans, and humans alone, were able to produce ... civilizations, making us by necessity interdependent, and the builders of our own destinies." (11)

REFERENCES

1. C. Schuchardt, Alfred Habdank Skarbek Korzybski: A Biographical Sketch, *General Semantics Bulletin* 3, Spring 1950, 2d printing (Englewood, NJ, Institute of General Semantics) 33-40.
2. A. Korzybski, *Manhood of Humanity* (Englewood, NJ, Institute of General Semantics, 2d ed. 1950) 111, 297-98.
3. S.I. Hayakawa, *Language in Thought and Action* (New York, Harcourt Brace Jovanovich, 4th ed. 1978) 12.
4. Ibid., 11.
5. Korzybski, *Manhood of Humanity*, 315.
6. Ibid., vi-vii.
7. Ibid., ix.
8. A. Korzybski, *Science and Sanity* (Englewood, NJ, Institute of General Semantics, 4th ed. 1958) lix.
9. Korzybski, *Manhood of Humanity*, xlviii.
10. R. Pula (Senior Editor of the *General Semantics Bulletin*, Lecturer for the IGS Summer Seminar Workshops), *General Semantics Seminar*, Album IV-D (San Diego, Educational Cassettes, 1979) six one-hour cassette tapes; available from the Institute of General Semantics or the International Society for General Semantics.
11. Korzybski, *Manhood of Humanity*, liv-lv.

From: *Et cetera* 47, no. 3 (Fall 1990) pages 300-302.

To a Poet a Thousand Years Hence

James Elroy Flecker
(1884-1915)

I who am dead a thousand years,
    And wrote this sweet archaic song,
Send you my words for messengers
    The way I shall not pass along.

I care not if you bridge the seas,
    Or ride secure the cruel sky,
Or build consummate palaces
    Of metal or of masonry.

But have you wine and music still,
    And statues and bright-eyed love,
And foolish thoughts of good and ill,
    And prayers to them who sit above?

How shall we conquer? Like a wind
   That falls at eve our fancies blow,
And old Maeonides the blind
   Said it three thousand years ago.

O friend unseen, unborn, unknown,
   Student of our sweet English tongue,
Read out my words at night, alone:
   I was a poet, I was young.

Since I can never see your face,
   And never shake you by the hand,
I send my soul through time and space
   To greet you. You will understand.

This poem, a favorite of S.I. Hayakawa (1906-1992) was read at his Memorial Gathering by his son, Alan Hayakawa. Dr. S.I. Hayakawa, a former United States Senator and a cofounder of *Et cetera* in 1943, published several general semantics books, including the recent 5th edition of the bestseller *Language in Thought and Action*, coauthored with his son Alan.

From *Et cetera* 50, no. 2 (Summer 1993) page 136.

In Pursuit of Safer Driving

by Gregory Sawin

IT CAN HAPPEN so easily: one moment you're a happy camper driving along as usual, and the next moment — screech — crunch — you have an accident that ruins your day. Should we be resigned to suffer these bad experiences because we believe they are unavoidable? Should we just believe that it's a matter of fate and when our number is up, it's up? If we believe this, then it is logical to think that how we drive makes no difference. "Either-or" thinkers seem to assume that they are either safe or doomed to have accidents and that they have no control over their fates. It would be more realistic for them to think in terms of probabilities: being safe drivers can reduce their chances of having accidents.

Links Between Thought and Action

Through training in general semantics, we become aware of connections between our thinking, acting, and the consequences. This view of how the world works is not compatible with fatalism. What happens to us *can* be influenced by our actions, and our actions *can* be guided by how we think.

General semanticists believe that if we can improve the quality of our thinking, our actions will more often fit the situation and we will have fewer unnecessary problems. Exploring two implications of the map-territory analogy will show that applying general semantics to driving can make us safer drivers.

Our thoughts are like maps that we use to navigate in the territories of our everyday life situations. (1,2) If there is a reasonably good match between our mental maps and the territory of our immediate surroundings, our behavior based on these maps generally should be more successful. However, even an accurate map represents only *some* parts of a territory: When we drive, whatever we discover about our situation at the moment comes to us through our senses, but they can take in only a sample of what is happening around us. We cannot know all about our driving situation; what we see *is not all* that is out there. If we are rational, we build our mental maps on the basis of what we can perceive. If we try to be more observant, we can cultivate greater awareness of the many happenings in each of our driving situations and we can be safer drivers. "According to the Traffic Safety Council, two of the top four causes of automobile accidents are inattention and improper lookout — in different terms, poor awareness." (3)

Awareness of Possibilities

We should drive on the basis of what we *see* and what to *expect*. First we use our senses to build mental maps of the facts around us. Then we can use our imagination to build additional maps that represent not facts, but possibilities — guesses about likely unseen factors in our driving situations. (4) For example, if I am on the verge of making a right turn where I can't see around the corner, I don't know what I'm getting into; yet I need some basis for deciding how to make the turn. If I am a thinking person, I can imagine a few possibilities and prepare for them; but if I am an unthinking person, I will just mindlessly drive into the unknown unprepared. I can take the turn fast, *assuming* that nothing will be in my way; or I can take the turn slowly, guessing that around the corner someone *could be* crossing the street, or that a car *could be* pulling out of a parking space along the curb, so I'm ready and able to stop just in case. If I take the turn slowly, I have more time to react to the emergence of an unseen hazard, so I'll have a chance to avoid an accident. However, if I take the turn fast, and someone gets in my way, then I won't be able to stop in time and I'll have little choice about what happens in the next horrifying moment. So be careful and try to get it right the first time. All too often in life, there is no second chance — you can't unscramble an egg.

Constant Change

Another point illustrated by the map-territory idea is that the territory is constantly changing, but the map doesn't change to keep up with the territory; so a map is out-of-date not long after it is made. The territory of a driving situation can change quickly, but our mental map based on our observations tends to remain unchanged unless we are constantly on the lookout for new information about our current situation. Checking and double-checking are the only ways to keep our mental maps as up-to-date as possible. But when we drive in a place where we have been hundreds of times before, it is easy to be caught off guard by a new obstacle. We may forget that each time is a unique experience — different people, different cars, different weather conditions — in short, different possibilities. Korzybski said that we live in a world of "... absolutely individual events, objects, [and] situations..." and he encouraged us to "...evaluate the individual happenings *uniquely*." (5) Just remember that "...everything around you is happening for the first time." (6)

A Potential Tragedy

Here's a true story about how I applied general semantics in one of my daytime driving situations. I had just turned onto a residential street where the road curved to the left on a slight dome-shaped hill. I was at the bottom of the hill and ahead of me at the top of the hill I could see a double-parked car that left room for only one lane of traffic for both directions. Between me and the double-parked car, on the other side of the street, someone was getting into a car. I couldn't see whether a car was coming from the other direction on the other side of the hill. If I had just *assumed* that it would be clear for me to drive through the one-lane space and then did so, I could have had a head-on accident or at least rammed other cars in swerving to avoid the oncoming car. The other driver might have swerved right into the person who was getting into a car. This tragedy could have happened if a car had come from the other direction and if I had just mindlessly assumed that what I could see was *all* there was to see. When I first came upon this scene, I stopped because I could imagine a few possibilities in this unique and potentially dangerous situation. At first, I refused to drive through the one-lane space, I just wanted to look for more clues to build a better mental map before making a decision.

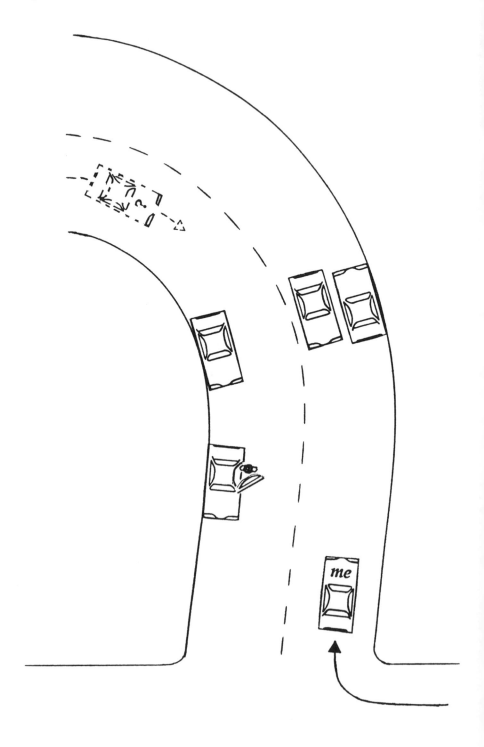

Having a good map of facts and possibilities as a basis for action would help me make a good decision and enable me to get it right the first time. Can you guess what happened while I studied the scene? Sure enough, a car came up the hill from the other direction, right through the one-lane space, and it did not come through slowly! After that car passed by me, I slowly approached the space so I could get a better look at what might be coming toward me and I was able to drive safely through it. In being able to avoid an accident, I felt richly rewarded for applying general semantics.

REFERENCES

1. F.P. Chisholm, *Introductory Lectures on General Semantics* (Englewood, NJ, Institute of General Semantics, 13th printing 1980) 35-40.
2. H.L. Weinberg, *Levels of Knowing and Existence* (Englewood, NJ, Institute of General Semantics, 2nd ed. 1973) 28-29 & 35.
3. K.T. Berger, *Zen Driving* (New York, Ballantine Books, 1988) 49.
4. Weinberg, *Levels of Knowing and Existence*, 15-25.
5. A. Korzybski, *Science and Sanity* (Englewood, NJ, Institute of General Semantics, 4th ed. 1958) 462.
6. Berger, *Zen Driving*, 42.

From *Et cetera* 47, no. 1 (Spring 1990) pages 82-84.

Can They Persuade You?

by Gregory Sawin

WHEN SOMEONE TRIES to sell you a product or change your mind, are you aware of the ways the persuader might be influencing you? Can general semantics help you evaluate a persuader's message?

General semantics is based on the view that we are "time-binders" — we bind together the past, present, and future.(1) We live in the present and learn from the past to prepare for the future; and we do this because our written and spoken languages give us tremendous communication power. In our everyday lives, as we plan for the future, we seek reliable information from others as the basis for decisions we make and actions we take.

Methods of Persuasion

Informational communication is intended to help the listener *learn* something, but persuasive communication is intended to lead the listener to *yield* to the persuader's point of view. (2)

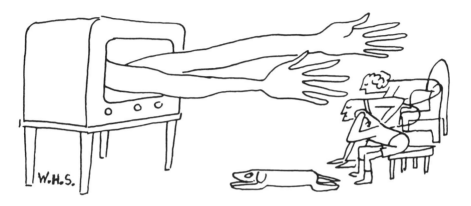

The commercial

One of the most common approaches in persuasive communication is to promise a reward and to connect the reward with use of the product. This appears to be one of the main functions of advertising; here are three examples: A Benson & Hedges cigaret ad shows a man singing and holding a cigaret. He is with a piano player and they are surrounded by an audience of attentive and admiring men and women. Another photo in this ad shows the singer, presumably just after his song, smoking the cigaret while the piano player looks on and smiles. The message in this ad seems to be "Smoke this cigaret and you will be the center of attention — you will be entertaining and popular." A Budweiser beer ad shows an aerial view of three sexy ladies in bathing suits who are stretched out side by side to bask in the sun on a big Budweiser-label towel. Their suits match different parts of the Budweiser label, so the suits blend into the label pattern of the towel they are lying on. The promoters of this beer apparently want the potential male customers to associate the Budweiser label with sex. The ad suggests that if you drink Budweiser, the ladies will come to you. A Newport cigaret ad says "Alive with Pleasure!" and shows a man standing in a pair of jeans while an attractive woman kneels and cuts away his jeans at mid-thigh to make cut-offs. This ad implies that smoking Newport will bring the smoker the pleasure of intimate fun with the opposite sex.

Such persuasive ads are applications of behavior modification principles. These ads may lead us to buy a product

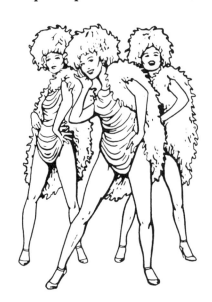

merely because it was shown with something we strongly desire, such as the "...loving admiration of voluptuous belles." (3) The persuaders are trying to sell products by hinting that using them will bring us fulfillment or emotional security, but these are not in the products. (4) Advertisers also persuade by connecting punishment with failure to use their products. For example, commercials for dandruff shampoos, underarm deodorants, and mouthwashes have portrayed non-users of their products as suffering embarrassment due to people noticing their dandruff flakes, body odor, or bad breath.

Misleading Maps

Some ads serve as maps that deliberately misrepresent territories. Such maps promise or threaten results in the territory that actually may be very unlikely to happen. General semanticists say that when you navigate by a false map, one that does not match the territory, you will not get to your destination — you will not get what you want. (5) Sometimes a persuader tries to program you with a false mental map that will influence your behavior. If you believe that map —

the hints or predictions that some of your needs will be satisfied as a result of buying a product — then you will probably act in the territory according to that map, meaning that you will buy the product. So, for those deceptive persuaders, it is not important to make the map correspond to the territory; what is important is that the customer *believes* the map and *buys* the product.

Some persuaders attempt to verbally hypnotize us so we will impulsively buy their products or accept their ideas regardless of whether we really need or want them. (6) For example, a Suzuki motorcycle ad that says "simply irresistible" seems designed to encourage the reader to make a quick decision to buy the motorcycle without shopping around to compare prices.

An unexpected effect of persuaders' tactics that repeatedly appeal to thoughtless, emotional, or impulsive decisions may be that such tactics will reshape and degrade our patterns of thinking for making serious decisions, such as whom to marry, when to buy a house, how to solve a problem, etc. (7) However, if we use general semantics, we may learn "delayed reactions" to avoid impulsive behavior by taking a moment to think twice about whether a statement makes sense or whether a course of action would improve a situation. (8)

Defending Ourselves Against Deception

General semanticists are concerned about persuaders trying to influence our thinking and behavior. Our destinies should not be decided by the persuaders. For Alfred Korzybski, the founder of general semantics, one purpose of this discipline is to help us learn more skills for navigating in our "verbal environments." (9) He wanted us to cultivate awareness of how we can more skillfully evaluate information and learn how the persuaders might lead us to act for their benefit, but not ours. (10)

In addition to manipulating our verbal environments, some advertisers are trying to reshape our *semantic environments* — they are trying to change our attitudes and values so we will buy their products. Korzybski said "Since commercialism cannot sell brains, but can sell trousers ... it establishes semantic standards whereby a man is evaluated by his clothes..." (11)

When we realize that a statement (map) may not correspond to the facts (territory), we may be inclined to delay our reactions to the statement and think about how likely it is that the statement matches the facts. The map-territory analogy and the principle of delayed reaction are two of the many general semantics tools we can use to separate sense from nonsense in our verbal environments. (12)

As we learn more about general semantics formulations, we expand our awareness of how communication can influence behavior. When we become more aware of how persuaders can manipulate our verbal and semantic environments, we can begin to defend ourselves against persuasion by thinking before acting. Hopefully this will lead to better decision-making and more satisfying results in our everyday lives.

REFERENCES

1. A. Korzybski, *Manhood of Humanity* (Englewood, NJ, Institute of General Semantics, 2nd ed. 1950) 59-60.
2. W.L. Schramm & D.F. Roberts (eds.), *The Process and Effects of Mass Communication* (Urbana, IL, University of Illinois Press, 1971) 43-44.
3. A. Bandura, *Principles of Behavior Modification* (New York, Holt, Rinehart & Winston, Inc., 1969) 600-601.
4. V. Packard, *The Hidden Persuaders* (New York, Washington Square Press/Pocket Books, 1957) 68.
5. A. Korzybski, *Science and Sanity* (Englewood, NJ, Institute of General Semantics, 4th ed. 1958) 58.
6. S.I. Hayakawa, *Language in Thought and Action* (New York, Harcourt, Brace, and Jovanovich, 4th ed. 1978) 106-107 & 255.
7. Ibid., Hayakawa, 257.
8. W. Johnson, *People in Quandaries: The Semantics of Personal Adjustment* (New York, Harper & Row, 1946; recent printing by the International Society for General Semantics, Concord, CA) 191-197 & 228-230.
9. A. Korzybski, *Science and Sanity*, 270.
10. Ibid., lxv, 295-296, 446 & 486.
11. Ibid., 519.
12. Ibid., 63, 78-84.

Also see: R.K. Goldsen, Why Television Advertising is Deceptive and Unfair, *Et cetera* 35, no. 4 (Winter 1978) 354-375.

From *Et cetera* 46, no. 2 (Summer 1989) pages 177-179.

Are We Arguing About The Same Thing?

by Gregory Sawin

W HEN PEOPLE ARGUE with each other, they apparently *assume* that they are arguing about the *same* thing. In an argument, each combatant is likely to operate in the either-or mode: "I know what I'm talking about, therefore I am right and you are wrong." In this mode, neither party is inclined to refrain from arguing long enough to ask questions and get answers that might clarify what each person is *really* talking about. I contend that, instead of exchanging views and perhaps reaching an understanding, people frequently and needlessly argue because each one fails to realize that his or her statement is about something different compared to the other person's statement. Arguments can become less frequent if people will apply some ideas from general semantics to help them make distinctions they usually do not make.

Five Key Ideas

A general semantics perspective can help us make the following distinctions:

28

1. The word is not the thing. "Say whatever you choose *about* the object, and whatever you might say *is not* it. Or, in other words: Whatever you might *say* the object 'is', well it *is not*."(l) This simply means that the object is not the words you use to describe it; no amount of words will make the object. This obvious advice is important because it requires us to make a sharp distinction between the silent level of the happenings around us and the level of words *about* these happenings. (2) Words are not as important as the facts they stand for; what a map tells you about a territory is not as important as the facts of the territory. The map is an abstraction from the territory, so the map necessarily leaves out many aspects of the territory. We can use a map to guide us, but ultimately it is the territory we have to cope with, not the map. Our descriptions about what we see and hear are based on our limited perceptual abilities; such statements are not absolutely true, complete, and objective. Talking is a mapping process that is ultimately about the observer's transaction with the observed. If I say, "Dogs are mean, but cats

are friendly," this reflects my experiences and biases; it is not an objective statement about dogs and cats. A statement results from someone's evaluation of something that is filtered through his or her senses and brain. Hayakawa put it this way: "human beings use extremely complicated systems... called *language*, with which they express and report what goes on in their nervous systems." (3)

2. Each person occupies a unique position in space-time, so each one has a unique point of view, literally. Eyewitnesses to the same car accident see it from different angles, and often they do not agree about how it happened.

3. No one can be absolutely objective in evaluating something. Each person's way of making sense of the world is shaped, in part, by his or her unique series of life experiences — the influences of culture, education, family and peer groups, rewarding or punishing experiences in daily life, etc. These constantly accumulating experiences form the basis or context for our judgments. Dawes claimed that "no observation or experience can take place outside of contexts." (4) Pemberton asserted that we carry our life histories around with us — these histories shape our ways of perceiving, judging, and speaking about new experiences. (5)

4. We should make a clear distinction between the relatively static, unchanging verbal level of words and the dynamic, constantly changing, nonverbal, process level of the happenings around us. According to Weinberg, "The map is static; the territory constantly flows. Words are always about the past or the unborn future, never about the living present. The present is ever too quick for them; by the time the words are out, it is gone." (6)

5. Regarding the verbal levels, we need to understand the difference between descriptions and inferences. A description refers to some thing or event that was observed, heard, etc. But Weinberg said, "An inferential statement is not limited by observation; it is a statement about that which has not been observed. It may be a guess which takes off from the point where observation ceases.... Thus, if I look out the

window, see water falling from the sky, and say, 'It is raining,' I have made a factual statement.... If I add that it is raining 1000 miles away, or around the corner, I am making an inference." (7) A prediction, such as "The sun will rise tomorrow," is also an inference, not a statement of fact, even though it may have a very high degree of probability of being correct. Strictly speaking, how can an event be a fact if it hasn't happened yet? (8)

In light of these distinctions, I see an important implication: Frequently, when people argue, they are not arguing about exactly the same thing. Arguments usually consist of conflicting statements, not about facts but about *evaluations*: feelings, attitudes, inferences, guesses, predictions, or value judgments regarding some thing, person, or situation. Dawes was referring to evaluation when he wrote, "The biologist, the environmentalist, the logger, the real estate developer, the artist, the nature lover, the child, the parent, and others who couldn't care less about trees, will each experience a tree differently, as a consequence of differences in perspectives, ... interests, ... etc. The immediate and usually overwhelming context of our own needs ... and concerns, often prevents us from remembering that there are other valid ... points of view." (9)

Unique Experiences

To illustrate how people might believe they are arguing about the same thing when they are actually arguing about different things, consider two friends of mine (each named Mona) and their attitudes about the comedian Woody Allen. Mona-1 hates him, but Mona-2 likes him. Their attitudes are subjective and result from their evaluation of the comic in light of each one's personal context: Mona-1 and Mona-2 grew up in very different environments. Each Mona developed a unique context or neuro-semantic environment (her inner world of meanings, her world-view, beliefs, attitudes, etc.) that influenced her judgment of Allen. (10) Not only does each Mona have a unique neuro-semantic environment, but each also had a unique series of exposures to Allen; it is very unlikely that both Monas saw exactly the same assortment of TV shows and movies that he appeared in. There would be no point in arguing because neither Mona would be speaking objectively about Woody Allen. Their different histories and different samples of his performances led them to generate different evaluations of him. Although their evaluations of him are in conflict, each opinion is probably justifiable and perhaps even logical, based on how each woman's particular life experiences shaped her way of looking at the world.

Map-Making

We are map-makers; we cope with events in our lives by making various kinds of maps of them. We make perceptual maps by using our senses to look, listen, etc. We create simple word-maps to describe what we sense, and we formulate idea-maps — inferences, generalizations, and conclusions that are based on our own experiences or on the reports of others. We construct all these mental maps in the context of our neuro-semantic environments. At each level of mapping, we must represent some factors in the map and leave out others. No one can be completely unbiased, objective, and all-knowing in making a map. As we grow up in particular environments, we learn to pay more attention to some things than to others, and to value some things more than others; this process of developing preferences and biases is unavoidable. Steve Allen wrote that "Everybody is biased and prejudiced. It is not even possible to grow up on Planet Earth without having to accept a good many ideas as true before we can possibly be mature enough to know if, in fact, they are true. There is no way to get around this." (11) We cannot prevent our biases from influencing how we make our maps, but we can become aware that we have such biases. Then, although we still cannot be truly objective, we may try to be less subjective by becoming aware of our mapping processes and by creating maps that correspond more accurately to what we really know.

Avoid Absolutes

Sometimes, a contributing cause of arguments is that people distort the facts by speaking in terms of absolutes. For example, unqualified statements such as "You *always* make a mess of things," "You *never* take me anywhere," or "*All* cats are friendly," are idea-maps that do not accurately represent the fact-territories. Such obvious inaccuracy invites a listener to argue with the person who made the statement. One way to reduce the likelihood of arguments is to speak more precisely — use qualifying terms such as "sometimes," "usually," "it seems to me that," "recently, I heard that," etc.

Each of us is a victim of our previous environments, and each develops a unique style of evaluating events. If we hear a remark that appears to conflict with our view, this should not be too surprising because we are hearing an evaluation from a unique person who has a personal history, values, and points of view that are not identical to those of any other individual. Bois wrote, "The wondrous thing is not that we disagree, but that we so often manage to get along passably well." (12)

REFERENCES

1. A. Korzybski, *Science and Sanity* (Englewood, NJ, Institute of General Semantics, 4th ed., 1958) 35.

2. W.H. Pemberton, *Sanity for Survival: A Semantic Approach to Conflict Resolution* (San Francisco, Graphic Guides, 1989) 14.

3. S.I. Hayakawa, *Language in Thought and Action* (New York, Harcourt Brace Jovanovich, 4th ed., 1978) 9.

4. M. Dawes, Multiordinality: A Point of View, *Et cetera* 43, no. 2 (Summer 1986) 131.

5. Pemberton, *Sanity for Survival*, 11-12, 68.

6. H.L. Weinberg, *Levels of Knowing and Existence: Studies in General Semantics* (Englewood, NJ, Institute of General Semantics, 2d ed., 1973) 35.

7. Ibid., 15-16.

8. Ibid., 19.

9. Dawes, Multiordinality, 132.

10. Korzybski, *Science and Sanity*, xxx, xlii, xliv, lxiv.

11. S. Allen, *Dumbth: And 81 Ways to Make Americans Smarter* (Buffalo, NY, Prometheus Books, 1989) 152-53.

12. J.S. Bois, *The Art of Awareness: A Textbook on General Semantics and Epistemics* (Dubuque, IA, William C. Brown, 3d ed. 1978) 34.

From *Et cetera* 48, no. 1 (Spring 1991) pages 91-95.

Taking Responsibility for the Meanings We Give: Part I

by Milton Dawes

Proposition 1

"WHENEVER WE AGREE or disagree with someone — or, to be more specific, with something — we have heard or read, we are to a great extent agreeing or disagreeing with 'ourselves.'" (I invite you to pause for a moment and take special notice of your reactions to this proposition at this time.) This proposition, at first hearing or reading, may seem to you to be a silly, irresponsible, and totally unacceptable thing for anyone to suggest. And you may also think that an idea such as this is designed simply to discourage genuine criticisms, undermine self-confidence, and put a damper on debates, discussions, and everyday conversations. I doubt that any of this will happen; but in any case, those are not my intentions. I am merely stating what seems to me to be a valid proposition, based on my acceptance, interpretations, and applications of some general semantics principles and formulations.

Proposition 2

The aim of Proposition 1 is mainly to provide supporting arguments for Proposition 2. Proposition 2 states that "If we are concerned to improve our relationships with our 'selves' and each other, and create healthier environments in our homes, in the places we work, and wherever we socialize, we could start by becoming more alert to how we as individuals contribute to and create the kinds of societies we live in, as a consequence of the ways we interpret and give meanings to our experiences. And since language constitutes a great deal of our thinking related to our everyday personal, social, and professional experiences and interactions, we could take more responsibility for the ways we interpret, and the meanings we give to, what we hear or read."

Specifically, we could take more responsibility for how we as individuals interpret and give meanings to what our experts, gurus, scientists, religious authorities, politicians, teachers, friends, reporters, writers, relatives, and others say or write. For the kinds of values we hold, the ways we relate to each other, and the kinds of societies we create for ourselves and our children are, to a great extent, based on the ways we interpret, and the meanings we give to, what we read and hear.

The Principle of Non-Identity

To return to Proposition 1: One of the general-semantics principles alluded to earlier is the "principle of non-identity."

This principle states that no two things are identical, that no things are absolutely the "same" in all respects. For example, even newborns labeled as "identical twins" are not absolutely identical — there are always some observable differences. The principle of non-identity further states that "In a world of change, growth, process, changing relationships...a thing is not even identical with itself." Now if things are not identical with themselves, if they are continuously changing ever so imperceptibly from moment to moment — changing position, changing relationships, changing internally, and so on — how can they ever be identical with each other?

The principle of non-identity is valid on both logical and empirical grounds. If any two things were the "same" in all respects, then, by definition and observation, they could not occupy or be seen to occupy two different space-time positions. If two things were identical (similar in all respects), we would not in any way be able to distinguish one from the other. We would not be able to point to one and say, "There is this one," then point to the other and say, "There is that one." To do that would be tantamount to admitting that one could be distinguished from the other and that they were seen in different places. But if each one occupied a different place, then their positional and functional relationships with other things would be different. So one could not honestly claim that they were the "same" in all respects.

We are strongly inclined, each one of us, to ignore these inescapable differences between the interpretations and meanings we give to what we hear and read, and the words, intentions, expectations, and meanings of a speaker or writer. If we accept the principle of non-identity, then the meanings and interpretations of a listener or reader cannot be identical with — cannot be the same as — the meanings of another individual, speaking or writing in a different place and at a different time. We choose, interpret, and understand words according to our individual life experiences — and we each have different life experiences. Of course we do understand each other, to a certain degree, and we can follow instructions reasonably closely. We are able to communicate mainly because our meanings have overlapping features. But except for those who claim to be mind-readers, our interpretations come between what is heard and read and what is said and written. To be fair to a speaker or writer, as listeners or readers, we should take some responsibility for the interpretations we make and the meanings we give to what we hear or read.

The Principle of Non-Allness

The principle of non-allness is another general-semantics principle advanced in support of Proposition 1. Briefly put, this principle states, "We cannot know, understand, become acquainted with, all of — nor say, describe, imagine,....all about anything," and this includes ourselves. The principle implies that, as interpreters, evaluators, and assigners of meanings, we cannot be absolutely certain of every aspect of our own evaluation processes; consequently, we cannot  be sure of the accuracy of our own interpretations, nor can we know all that's behind the words of others. Accepting and remembering the principle of non-allness, we have the responsibility at least to make allowances for the possibility of errors, misevaluations, and misinterpretations. It is our responsibility to remind ourselves that all was not said or written, and that all could not have been said or written. It is our responsibility to remember that any interpretation we make, any meaning we give to what we hear or read, is based on very small samplings of whatever else could have been said or written. And it is our responsibility to remind ourselves that our agreements as well as disagreements are based on our evaluations of our interpretations of these small samplings.

The General Principle of Uncertainty

This principle is more general than Heisenberg's principle of uncertainty. It states, "Living as we do, in a dynamic world of change, growth, process, etc., and in a world where no two things, situations, etc., are identical, the 'truth' value of the relatively static and general statements we make should be evaluated in terms of *degrees of probability* ranging from impossibility to certainty." As an exercise, how, for instance, would you evaluate the truth value of the following statements? (The first one was heard in a bank.) "I pay back my loan the way I want." "He is on the permanent staff." "Till death do us part." "Do you swear to tell the truth, the whole truth, and nothing but the truth?" "Your car will be ready tomorrow." "Five hundred dollars cash back."

If you refer to what was mentioned above regarding the principles of non-identity and non-allness, you may notice that these two principles (among others) "make" a general principle of uncertainty inexorable. The principle of non-identity implies that to understand anything there have to be some prior interpretations. And, following this, we cannot be absolutely sure that what we understand is precisely what was meant. The principle of non-allness implies that all our understanding is based on limited analysis of limited input of limited information. So we cannot be absolutely sure that the way we have interpreted a statement precludes all other possible interpretations. (The "allness" — that is, all our understanding — in the above statement and implied in other general-semantics principles is not a contradiction or paradox if one includes a date.)

The principle of uncertainty, together with those of non-identity and non-allness, "suggest" that we develop in ourselves certain attitudes, habits, orientations, approaches in our conversations, discussions, listenings, and readings. Such a habitual approach would include the following considerations: (1) We cannot *not* interpret, we cannot *not* make assumptions. (2) We should expect some degree of inaccuracy in our interpretations — based as they are on our individual experiences, standards, assumptions, beliefs, and training. (3) We should acknowledge these inaccuracies, assumptions, and uncertainties as unavoidable aspects of our communication processes.

In support of this "uncertainty approach," we could change our agreement or disagreement responses to something along the following lines: "As far as I know; as much as I understand; based on the little information I have; not knowing what was left out; realizing that I had to make a few guesses and projections; I agree (or disagree) with my own interpretations of this that I am hearing (or reading); furthermore, since I do not expect people to say or write 'meanings' instead of 'words,' I take responsibility for the meanings I give to whatever I hear or read." (Remember, we are talking about an attitude, so we don't have to actually say the above.)

The societies we have inherited, help to create, and to a great extent support, do not usually encourage values pertaining to uncertainty and probability. So it is understandable if at this point you find that your thoughts include such words and phrases as *ludicrous, idealistic, academic, philosophical, nothing would ever get done.* We have been conditioned to believe, we are inclined to believe, and we have abundant evidence that leads us to believe that a person with an uncertainty approach will be seen, described, thought of, and treated something like this: "She or he is the kind of person who is unsure of herself or himself; can't be relied upon; is wimpish; splits hairs; lacks self-confidence; seems a weak character or a fence sitter; cannot make decisions."

Despite our social and cultural conditionings, we can also consider the following positive aspects of uncertainty. The principle of uncertainty is not an absolute law of the universe, stating what must occur, what we must do at every single instant of our existence. Without some degree of certainty, there would be no science or mathematics as we know them. To recognize a principle of uncertainty is to learn to live our lives with a certain *degree of uncertainty*. In a world of change, process, and diversity, to be always certain is to be at a disadvantage. Following a map of certainty will sooner or later lead one up a path to increasing distress, while being uncertain helps us to acknowledge errors and seek improvements. Being certain discourages creative approaches to solving problems; it promotes intolerance, prejudices, conflicts, and violence. Without doubts, there would be little advancement in knowledge. A recognition of the possibility of uncertainty helps us to accept more responsibility for our guesses, expectations, theories, and opinions. An individual or society that has no doubts about its certainties will sooner or later discover, to its dismay, that the world around it, and the people it encounters, cannot always be relied upon to meet its expectations.

From *Et cetera* 48, no. 1 (Spring 1991) pages 96-101.

"General semantics encourages the study of processes behind the curtain of language. It investigates the relations between words, what words refer to and the human beings involved, the effects of the language on evaluation and of evaluation on language."

—Mary Morain

Taking Responsibility for the Meanings We Give: Part II

by Milton Dawes

Words as Variables

T HERE ARE OTHER general semantics premises and formula-tions that could be cited in support of Proposition 1. For now, those mentioned above will suffice. Let's return for a moment to Proposition 1: "Whenever we agree or disagree with something we have heard or read, we are to a great extent agreeing or disagreeing with ourselves." The "truth" value of this proposition has very little to do with whether one person is right and another wrong, or whether what is heard or read can be shown to be true or false. The "truth" value of the proposition has to be evaluated in terms of interpretations, understandings, and meanings, not in terms of facts per se.

Apart from the premises referred to, Proposition 1 can be supported using the mathematical notion of "the variable." The variable has been defined as "a symbol that can represent any one of a set of values." Words can be considered as "semantic variables." In terms of process, time, space, con-

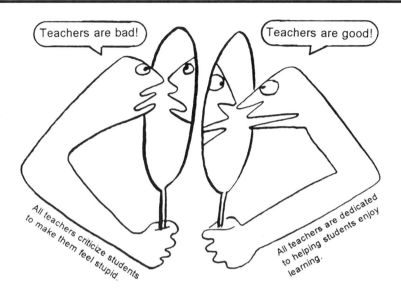

W.H. Schneider cartoon adapted by G. Sawin

text, frame of reference, interpreters (anything, for that matter) can be thought of in terms of variables. Any thing, situation, experience, or event is usually given a wide variety of interpretation and meaning values. As an unavoidable consequence of our unique life experiences, words mean different things to each of us. If you can recall situations where you thought you were misquoted or misunderstood, or followed directions to an unfamiliar place, or struggled with an instruction manual, you will have a good understanding of words as variables.

Interpreting: An Automatic Process

We are not usually aware that we give our own meaning values to our experiences, or to what we hear or read. We make interpretations and give meanings without being aware that we are doing so. We are constantly making interpretations — it is an automatic process. Our nervous systems seem to work more efficiently by not requiring us, at self-conscious levels, to be constantly engaged in observing that we are making interpretations. Try to imagine what it would be like if every time we had an experience, or heard or read something, we immediately became aware that we were in a process of interpreting! This awareness would now in its turn become an experience to be interpreted. And this new awareness.... get the picture? This extreme, self-reflexive mode of interpreting our experience of interpreting would probably put us in a trance-like state. It would be very difficult to make decisions or act.

The complexities of modern living require us to become more mindful of the fact that we interpret and give meanings. As diverse societies and cultures come together; as individuals and groups speaking different languages meet, intermix, and interact; as individuals with different training and skills communicate and work with each other — their different meaning-based values clash. Not unexpectedly, confusions, prejudices, tensions, and conflicts tend to increase.

Increasing our awareness that things are not what we say they are, that the meanings we give to our experiences and to situations we find ourselves in are uniquely our meanings, that words mean different things to different people, would do much to lower tensions, clarify differing viewpoints, and improve the quality of our relationships with ourselves and each other.

No Direct Access to Meanings

We have no direct way of knowing what others mean by their words. We have no way of bypassing the intrusive, selective, differentiating, integrating, representational processes of our nervous systems. Nor do we presently have any way of knowing how much, and to what degree, we may or may not have added to, subtracted from, reconstructed, reshaped, distorted, or created any such meaning. How can we know how much our fears, hopes, expectations, prejudices, or values have contributed to the particular ways we observe, think about, and respond to situations? If we can't be sure that what we understand is what was meant, shouldn't we take some responsibility for the meanings we give?

Exploring "Meaning"

If we are to take responsibility for the meanings we give to what we read or experience, it would be helpful to do some explorations into the realms of meaning. Such explorations would deepen our understandings of meaning and sharpen our sensitivities to the importance of meaning in diverse areas of our everyday living. What follows is a very brief account of some of my explorations. The statements, however else they must be interpreted, should not be taken as conclusions but rather as propositions. They represent some aspects of what meaning means to me at the time of writing. Dictionaries give the "meanings" of words through references to other words. But remembering the times we have felt hurt, angry, put down, encouraged, or complimented by what someone said or wrote, we suspect that meanings have more to do with our lives than merely with other words in a dictionary.

"Meaning" is a high-order abstraction label for our attempts to build bridges between what we know (or think we know) and what we know we don't know — bridges between the data that come to us through our senses and whatever else we suspect is going on in and around us. Our unceasing and pervasive search for meanings provides us with undeniable clues — messages from "ourselves" to "our-selves" — that we do not know it all.

Meaning represents our search for patterns that would provide us with some sort of continuity between events and our experiences, in different times and different places. Meaning has to do with our individual attempts to make sense of what we experience going on in our inner and outer worlds. We look for relationships, patterns, and connections to satisfy our need to know and understand what's going on; we look for clues that will help us get along better, obtain what we want, avoid problems, lessen stress, improve performance, and make better plans and decisions.

Nothing in or of itself has meaning. No thing, event, experience, situation, or word is its own meaning. Meanings cannot be divorced from interpretations and interpreters. The meaning or meanings of anything will not be found in the thing. The meaning of a sound, painting, piece of music, dream, or statement will not be found in the sound, or music, or statement. If the meaning of a thing was a part of the thing, how would we know where the "meaning" ended and the thing began? "Meaning" refers to processes in *psychophysiological* environments. Features of these environments include curiosity, surprise, anger, prejudice, opinions, beliefs, humor, fear, attitudes, values, and so on. Meaning does not exist in geographical environments as such; we cannot point to a meaning.

Each one of us creates our own meanings. And since each of us has our own unique ways of seeing, experiencing, and thinking about things and situations, no two of us will give the same meanings to situations we find ourselves in or to words we have heard or read. In view of all this, it would seem more reasonable for us to ask, "What does this mean to me?" than to ask, "What does this mean?"

Because words do not have meanings in themselves, we attempt to bridge the enormous gap between what we hear or read and what is intended by a speaker or writer. Frequently, we confuse and identify what we feel and understand, generated by what we hear or read, with whatever message a speaker or writer intended to convey.

In a world of infinite numbers of relationships, where everything (as far as we know) is dynamically interrelated with other things, a world where not all of these relationships are known or can be known, human meanings (despite our tendencies to hang onto the familiar and traditional) cannot be final or complete. As we get to know more about ourselves, our world, and ourselves-in-our-world, what things mean to us changes. As we see more, hear more, travel to new places, meet and talk with people, and acquire skills, the ways we "see" things change — despite our beliefs that we are the "same" persons.

If we accept that situations, behaviors, or statements do not have meanings in and of themselves, then we cannot reasonably and responsibly say that anything is "meaningless." Saying that something is meaningless is another way of saying that it does not mean anything to us at this time. We can, if sufficiently motivated, make sense of and give meanings to anything we choose.

Because meaning has to do with our deep need to find continuity and consistency in ourselves and in our worlds, the meanings we give are interrelated, integrated, and coordinated. The meanings we give to our experiences, or to what we hear or read, depend a great deal on the meanings we have given both to other experiences and to other things we have heard and read. This integration and consistency of meanings makes it extremely difficult for us to change attitudes, prejudices, beliefs, values, and behaviors, even when we realize that it is to our advantage to do so.

Recognizing that meaning is so vital in all areas of our lives, that things are not what we or others say they mean, that we have the inalienable option to change our interpretations as we please, could greatly increase our levels of self-confidence and personal power. We could accelerate our personal development, increase our intelligence, and improve our personal and professional relationships by being more sensitive to, more sensible about, and more responsible for the ways we interpret and the meanings we give to our experiences and to what we hear or read. "Easier said than done," you may be thinking. (Since I said it myself, I agree with me.) As mentioned before, making interpretations and giving meanings are basically automatic processes. But with some practice, we can become more aware of these goings-on. It requires catching ourselves doing such things as explaining, giving opinions, criticizing, expecting things to happen in particular ways, and agreeing and disagreeing.

Meaning plays an enormous role in our lives. To repeat, meaning is not just a matter of words. Our values, prejudices, beliefs, sciences, philosophies, religions, and artistic activities are based on meanings. We live our lives in terms of meanings. The kinds of societies we create and support develop from the interpretations and meanings we give to our experiences, especially to what we hear and read. "Meanings," to a great extent, direct our lives. But since we are capable, to some degree, of recognizing, reviewing, and modifying our interpretations, we can also direct our meanings to some extent.

The Guessing Game

Let's return once again to Proposition 1: Whenever we agree or disagree with something we heard or read, we are to a great extent agreeing or disagreeing with ourselves. How do you now feel about Proposition 1? Do you agree? If your answer is 'Yes,' here is another question. What are you agreeing or disagreeing with — the words as you have read them or the words as you now understand them? Suppose Proposition 1 were expressed in a foreign language with words you could pronounce but did not understand. Would you agree or disagree? If you are still puzzled, here is how I arrived at Proposition 1.

When I read or listen to someone speaking, I am aware (sometimes) that I do not and cannot know what message or messages the words are intended to convey. I am aware (sometimes) that I do not know the feelings, expectations, motives, or attitudes represented by the words. So I make some guesses (without necessarily being aware that I am doing this). I arrive at some understanding based on my past experiences as well as my present beliefs and expectations. (This takes place at non-self-conscious levels.) My agreement or disagreement expresses my evaluation of my understanding. (This I am sometimes aware of.)

If you disagree with the communication processes as outlined above (as you understand from the words), consider this: How comfortable would you be if you knew that anyone could "read your mind" and know exactly what you were thinking or feeling? It certainly would be a different kind of world, "don't you think?"

Taking Responsibility

If we could read each other's minds directly and completely, our human worlds would probably be healthier places. But as this is not the case, we'll have to do the best with what we have. As far as we know, our communication processes necessarily involve interpretations. Based on our interpretations, we arrive at meanings. Our meanings are expressed through our feelings, attitudes, prejudices, beliefs, values, etc. The kind of society we help to create and support, our relationships, our social institutions, and so on, all depend on our attitudes, beliefs, values, and the like. We are not animals. We do not live our lives entirely according to instinctive urges. Our societies are based on interpretations and meanings. We have some measure of control over the ways we interpret things. With a certain degree of alertness, we can recognize and, if necessary, review, modify, and change our interpretations. We are self-reflexive beings. We have the abilities to correct and improve our interpretations toward probable higher "truth" values.

It is easy for us to blame the politicians, the system, the corporations, the media — anyone but ourselves — for our social and other problems. We don't usually acknowledge the parts we play — how we, through the meanings we give, contribute to the problems we complain about. We could put much more effort into improving our thinking toward becoming more critical thinkers and interpreters. Applying such general-semantics principles as non-identity and non-allness could help us a great deal to improve our thinking about our thinking. We need to ask "our-selves" more often the question, "How do I know that what I believe is so?" For our own well-being, we need to remind "our-selves" more often that there are intrinsic differences between what we believe and what is going on.

From *Et cetera* 48, no. 3 (Fall 1991) pages 329-335.

Silent Knight: Protecting Yourself with Silence

by Dennis Reuter

IT WAS A BEAUTIFUL SPRING MORNING and the radio weatherman promised clear skies, so my wife made a picnic salad from a new recipe and off we went to the "Bach in the Park" concert advertised in the paper.

While waiting for the music to start, we tried the salad. Although the recipe had promise, the salad had a bitter, disagreeable taste. Then a rock band started playing modern arrangements of Bach's works — badly. Finally it started raining — hard.

How can we stay happy and balanced when reality is so different than our expectations? Is there a way to protect ourselves from stressful over-reaction, disappointment, and frustration? I would like to recommend one method.

Decades ago, Alfred Korzybski advocated the use of silence to protect us from emotional pain and discouragement. (1) "Silence" in this context refers to an inner experience of nonverbal awareness, not the lack of noise in the outer environment. It includes a realization that our lives involve several

W.H. Schneider cartoon adapted by G. Sawin

levels of activity, some of which are unspeakable or "silent." Practicing silence we may avoid the development of strong expectations, rapidly adjust to unforeseen events, and ease the pain caused by emotional over-reaction.

To understand how silence can be so beneficial we must briefly review the way our nervous system creates maps of reality, and how the different phases of that process relate to each other.

Reality and the Human Nervous System

Human life is integrated within "reality," and our view of that reality is shaped by the nature of our human nervous system. To over-simplify, we live our lives on three basic levels of activity:

1) "reality"
2) experience
3) maps

Although I describe them here separately, these three stages are phases of one process and not truly separate. Using various aspects of my picnic as an example, let's look at these three levels, then see how practicing silence provides psychological protection from our reactions to unexpected events.

"Reality" includes the electro-magnetic structure of the universe, the atomic and molecular formation of our nervous system, activity of the body's hormones and neurotransmitters, sub-atomic processes, etc.

At my picnic, this included the radio waves carrying the weather report and the complex interaction of moisture, heat, and electrical patterns involved in "weather"; the electro-chemical interaction of the salad with the tongue; and the vibrations in the air made by musical instruments.

The next phase, our "experience" of reality, involves our feelings and senses. Examples are our emotional reactions, moods, intuitions; what we see-taste-touch-hear-smell; our pains and pleasures, etc. (2) These experiences are unique and private to each of us, not capable of being shared directly with others.

At the picnic, examples include the feel of cold rain on the face; the taste of the salad; and the sound of the music. It also includes anger at the weatherman; the sensation of unsatisfied hunger; and keen disappointment about the music.

Finally, the third stage of the process is "maps" — what we say and think *about* our experience and *about* reality. This encompasses words, symbols, ideas, beliefs, expectations, and inferences. Our strong opinions about right and wrong are also part of this level.

Specifically, in relation to the picnic, it includes the weatherman's spoken words; the written recipe for the salad; and the newspaper ad for the concert. It also includes my expectations that the weather would be clear, the salad savory, and the music pleasant.

Because the human nervous system is self-reflexive, this level also includes inferences based upon our opinions and evaluations about our beliefs. Conclusions that the weatherman is unreliable; that my wife is a bad cook; and that the musicians are inept are all part of the "maps" level of activity.

Taken to extremes, those conclusions could include that "because we cannot trust what someone says, life is unfair"; that "my wife is an unworthy woman requiring a divorce"; and that "the musicians, by desecrating a great composer, deserve to be shot."

Relations Among the Three Phases

While the third phase of the process is verbal or symbolic, the first two are silent and unspeakable. (3) Furthermore, we actually live our lives entirely on the unspeakable levels. The verbal level is auxiliary, and effective only when translated into an action, a feeling, or some other event on the silent, unspeakable levels. (4)

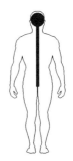

Because of the way the human nervous system functions, these three phases occur in a certain order — reality first, experience next, maps last. This process repeats itself instant after instant. Additionally, these phases also interact with each other, one level affecting the other two. This explains how our beliefs or expectations can affect our emotional reactions, brain chemistry, and health.

When we react to life, we are reacting to some or all of these three main divisions. But, because of the constant repetition and continual interaction of the phases, the underlying order is often overlooked or lost in the shuffle. This can lead to confusion, over-reaction, heartache, anger, stress, and harmful neuro-transmitter activity.

Because the weatherman promised clear skies, I expected them (map). The rain (reality) and its dampness (experience) contradicted that expectation, and I became upset. Similarly with the salad and the music. How does silence protect us from this type of self-induced distress?

Practicing silence focuses awareness on the dynamic nature of reality and away from dogmatic attachment to our  beliefs and expectations. Such a focus breaks the emotional reaction we have when reality and expectations conflict. Expecting clear skies is useless when the rain starts falling. We cannot read a recipe to nourish our bodies, nor look at sheet music to hear a symphony being played.

To react properly to the many events in our lives, we must be aware of the three different levels described above, but with more weight being given to the silent levels than to our beliefs or expectations about the event. (5) Giving too much value to our maps and inferences often gives rise to over-emotional activity and unclear thinking. Korzybski maintained that practicing silence on the unspeakable levels affects all of our psychological reactions and regulates them to the benefit of the organism-as-a-whole. (6)

Silence introduces a delay in our actions by curbing the tendency to form rapid conclusions and inferences. (7) With silence, a more balanced evaluation follows; reactions based on that evaluation are more appropriate, sane, and healthy.

Had I given less value to the words of a weatherman, my adverse reaction to the rain would have been lessened. Had I waited to see what the salad tasted like, my expectations would not have been frustrated. My strong opinion that classical music is the best kind prevented a neutral emotional response to the rock band.

Because the unspeakable levels are so influential and important in our lives, experiencing those levels is also important. To experience the unspeakable levels requires practice on those levels — there is no verbal, "intellectual" way to do it. Therefore, it is crucial to cultivate silence as an actual neurological activity. How is this done?

Techniques for Cultivating Silence

The practice of silence involves temporarily not thinking and not speaking, even inwardly in self-talk. To cultivate this, we can begin with common objects, such as a pen or chair. Because of the interaction between neurological activity and psychological functions, training with objects outside our skin automatically affects the difficult-to-reach "feeling-thinking" reactions inside the skin. (8)

Look at the chosen object, touch and handle it if you wish, but remain silent outwardly *and* inwardly. (9) Do not speak, label it, describe it, talk to yourself, or "think" about it. In the beginning, you may find this can be done for only a second or two at a time. With practice, the duration will increase.

Another technique, similar to the above but involving the body, is an ancient meditation practice. As you breathe, focus attention on a place inside the nostrils where the air passes in and out. Remaining silent within and without, simply observe the sensation of air passing by that spot. If you find yourself thinking, gently return attention to your breathing. Do this for five minutes each day.

This approach can be taken one step further by focusing attention upon a mood or feeling, such as "anger," "fear," or "joy." (10) During these times, stop talking and start focusing on the way that activity *feels*. Do not label it with words, nor think about why it is present. Remain emotionally impassive, neither for nor against the feeling, and dwell in the experience as an impartial observer. (11)

These relaxation and stress-reduction exercises benefit the body, psyche, and relationships with others. Medical reports consistently point out the advantages brought by a calm response to daily stress.

A final technique, which develops control on the unspeakable levels themselves, might be called "Touch and Let Go." This involves writing down a word, phrase, or description of some uncomfortable event. It can be any person or situation that causes discomfort or stress.

Look at the words, reflect upon the situation, saying or thinking anything you want about it. Then touch the paper and become silent, inside and out; do not talk to yourself or "mentally" consider the event. Experience the uncomfortable *feeling* the event usually produces, not the reasons for it.

Then remove your hands from the written words while you also release the tension and anxiety you have created. Imagine the feeling of being free from the influence of the event. By this practice you are gaining some control over that situation and increasing your awareness of the silent levels of life.

By applying silence in these ways, a new component enters our psychological make-up. Our evaluations and reactions become more healthy, appropriate, and constructive. Control over our automatic reactions improves. Options appear that were previously blocked by over-stimulation and under-evaluation.

These exercises use silence to build an inner poise which protects us in difficult times. Silence is a major cornerstone for sane living and personal security, but is difficult to attain without practice. We can talk about silence and discuss its merits, but unless it is actually practiced, there are no substantial benefits. (12)

This is not an "all or nothing" approach — learning to be silent is developed by degrees. To the extent that it is practiced and acquired, to that degree there are benefits.

In this regard, achieving silence is like learning to type or play a musical instrument. Any effort is rewarded, and persistent practice over time assures success.

REFERENCES

1. A. Korzybski, *Science and Sanity: An Introduction to Non-Aristotelian Systems and General Semantics* (Englewood, NJ, Institute of General Semantics, 4th ed. 1958) 416-18.
2. Ibid., 477.
3. Ibid., 34.
4. Ibid., 35, 478-9.
5. Ibid., 176-7, 202 & 317.
6. Ibid., 35.
7. Ibid., 357, 422 & 424.
8. Ibid., 34.
9. Ibid., 637.
10. Ibid., 328-29.
11. Ibid., 329.
12. Ibid., 35, 328-29, 416, & 477.

From *Et cetera* 48, no. 4 (Winter 1991-1992) pages 434-439.

Escape From a Frozen Universe: Discovering General Semantics *

by Paul Dennithorne Johnston

W HY DID THEY CONFUSE ME? For years I listened, occasionally with acute distress, as people voiced conflicting views — each claiming to describe social reality and moral necessity. With my discovery of general semantics came an explanation for this frustrating disparity of "knowledge" as propounded by different individuals and a method of interpretation for solving many problems of the social world and the self.

Why does one person tell me one thing *is* fact, or truth or right, and another tell me exactly the opposite? Lacking reliable information, how can one negotiate a complex society

without repeatedly making mistakes? General semantics has helped me come to terms with these discouraging riddles.

To Be or Not To Be a Writer

When at 15 I first sold a short story, I decided I had to *be* a writer. At that time, our family lived on a schooner in the Bahama Islands. We had moved there from the Massachusetts countryside in my ninth year. I grew up isolated from urban society and did not experience city life until leaving home at 17. Subsequently, I often felt confused by the social world and its diversity of cultural values. Although I often had difficulty establishing common ground with the reading public, I continued to try to *be* a writer.

Publishers bought my short stories but rejected my first 10 novels. I despaired of earning a living writing fiction and thought I *was* a failure. As a reporter or editor, I could earn a living, but, according to my idea, that did not constitute *being* a writer. Therefore I had failed to *be* what I had set out to *be*.

With hindsight, I see that general semantics would have eased my burden by helping me view differently the idea of *being*, to see *being* as a kind of epistemological problem, instead of a notion of a fixed state of existence finally achieved, a logical construct having unfortunate real-life repercussions on my self-image and my happiness.

Either-Or

Like many English-speaking people, I had learned an Aristotelian system of reasoning with which I perceived the world in terms of opposites: a thing *was*, or it *was not*; I thought in terms of black-white, beautiful-ugly, good-bad, dead-alive and so on. My parents had given me values mostly from the 19th-century Romantics: "Truth," "Beauty," "Art," "Culture," "Knowledge," etc. I had read voraciously, and I tended to see the world through the eyes of English literature. At home I had learned absolute good-bad dichotomies, for example: GOOD: literature, originality, individuality, abstinence; BAD: television, mass production, conformity, drunkenness. According to my logical system of polar opposites, which inherently followed Aristotle's law of the excluded middle, either *I am a writer* or *I am not a writer*. My statement "I am a writer" seemed fraudulent to me because I had to earn a living doing other things. My on-off logic allowed no middle way, no *degrees of being a writer*.

I got my first job in Nassau, a city where the "decadence" of night clubs, bars, brothels and casino gambling shocked my innocent sensibilities, as the materialism and disrespect for "culture" that I saw conflicted with my idealized picture of

reality. Meanwhile, I felt some contempt for the "respectable" class because it practiced conformity. Attempts to rebel against my sheltered upbringing, my going to parties, bars and night clubs, often produced conflicting feelings: guilt and a desire to break free of puritanical inhibitions.

A few years later, to develop my writing skills, I worked as a reporter in England. There, in a country where one's native accent apparently decided one's financial and social status, I also perceived confusing messages on how life should *be*, particularly from that war of values between the classes. Attitudes between upper and lower classes seemed quite "racist," all the more bewildering to me because the "race" (social classes) had the same color skin. While employed varnishing rowing sculls at an elite boarding school, I observed an elderly white lower-class male kowtow to an upper class white schoolboy, a child of under 10: avoiding eye contact, the old man hung his head obsequiously, touched his forelock and muttered "Sir." Observation of this event left me feeling stunned with disbelief.

Seeking the Truth

At 33, after jobs as clerk, book-keeper, reporter, editor, railway porter, farm worker, carpenter, and so on, I went to college in London. I thought if I could learn the *truth* about reality, my confusion would disappear.   Studying sociology, psychology, and philosophy felt like I had found a supermarket of Truths, every Truth the *Real* Truth, and every one different.

I learned about Truth as a relationship, not a thing. At last I had found the truth about Truth! *If objective truth does not exist, we view the world subjectively. We negotiate the truth. The most powerful negotiator wins.*

I learned that language "bewitches" people. (1) One asks, "Is it the truth?" and searches for "the truth" as if it exists. The structural logic of language tricks one into thinking a thing exists when it does not. My conclusion: Knowledge does not equal truth and reality. Disciplines, doctrines and philosophies might have internal truth, as closed formal systems, yet still remain essentially meaningless. *We experience life autistically, deluded that we communicate.*

In my search for definitions, I had written news stories, plays, humor, essays, articles, poetry, short stories, novels. I had belonged to an institution that gave its own slant to the truth and called it news. Although academics and philosophers had more sophisticated ideas, they also looked through their own spectacles, and said this *is* this and that *is* that, without agreement among themselves.

Words do not speak truth; words create the brand of truth required. Words exhort, persuade, categorize, define. Words lie. So I felt.

I still wanted a universal truth, mediator, designer, etc. I wanted the world to "make sense."

I still felt that words and meaning had great significance; I thought if I could see through cultural bias and discover *how we know what we know,* I would find *the* answer. I enrolled for post-graduate study of the sociology of knowledge at the University of Wales, departed London, and bought a small-holding in Wales, five acres, a house, and barn. However, when the university term began, I chose to remain on the farm and continue writing. My pursuit of Truth had led nowhere. The tautological basis of knowledge meant that nobody knew anything. I might as well stay at home and milk the goats.

E-Prime

A few years later in California Dr. Ed Kellogg told me about E-Prime, an English variant that eliminates the use of the verb *to be* in all its forms. He showed me his manuscript of an article about E-Prime and we discussed the subject at length.

E-Prime excited me because it offered an escape from the tyranny of the "is of identity," a way of *being* that translated a dynamic universe into a frozen condition which meant no growth, little joy in learning experience, and fear of change. For example, a person who *is* a writer must live up to a preconceived notion of *being* and *continue to exist as such,* or fail. Conventional logic allowed me no escape from the frustration of not being what I should *be.* However, eliminating the verb *to be* increased my freedom to experience both the world and the self as *process.* In addition, one obtained increased freedom from the tendency to force living experience into static conceptual boxes, a paradoxical need rarely satisfied because life-experience consists of endless change.

Later, Dr. Kellogg gave me a copy of *Et cetera* with his E-Prime article in it. (2) I read every article in that *Et cetera,* and mailed my application for International Society for General Semantics membership.

Conflicting Realities

As I read more about general semantics, my enthusiasm grew. Korzybski's model of *abstracting* explained to me that people "know" different realities as they *abstract different pieces of a vast dynamic universe,* and it explained why people of equal intelligence, education and ability hold such different beliefs.

The problem of conflicting realities had long troubled me. In this article, I use the term *realities,* rather than *value-system,* to suggest that most people possess little awareness of their immersion in a particular system. To them (and to me) there appears no choice of viewpoint, values or "fact"; *it is the way it is.* My early reality I learned from my family. I valued certain abstractions: nature, "good" taste, self-control, thrift, work, individualism, literature, art, etc., and distrusted others: artificiality, vulgarity, materialism, hedonism, waste, laziness, conformity, crowds, "the system," etc.

In Nassau, in my late teens, I had found new "rules." People took pride in their ability to have a good time. A few years later, when I moved to England, I saw another set of realities, conflicting rules between the classes and within classes. The middle class valued abstractions of refinement, proper behavior, good character, honor, justice, fair play, respectability. The working class seemed to hold in contempt many middle-class ideals, and to value, on the one hand, independence and "being clever" rather than education or infrastructure, and, on the other hand, security through loyalty to their "betters."

I heard working-class people use a vocabulary of absolutes, often spoken with great conviction, a vocabulary of *it is*. By contrast, middle-class speakers often used the relativistic terms "rather," "perhaps," "as it were," etc. Nevertheless, "correct" middle-class attitudes and behavior had the importance of a moral imperative: "It isn't done," "It's not proper," etc.

Not thoroughly schooled in the reality of either class, I sometimes did not know what to think or do. I felt trapped by the absolutisms of my upbringing and by those of my new environment, and I could imagine no escape.

One profound difference between my reality and the British reality lay in the attitude toward individual potential. In an American elementary school I had learned the democratic ideal; I recall my first-grade teacher telling us, "Anyone can grow up to be president." My ancestors left Britain and Ireland to escape the personal and economic oppression of a stratified society. In Canada, my grandfather took his family west to homestead virgin territory. The "pioneering spirit" permeated my own experience of our family's move to isolated islands in the Bahamas. With my North-American belief in individuality, I could not accept the English view that a person should never try to "rise above his station."

General Semantics

Thus, the general semantics theory that we abstract *what we think we know* explained to me the source of conflicting realities and removed many doubts about my own ability to perceive the social world. As I studied, I sought to remain aware that my own perceptions come from abstracting. I began using general semantics principles in my daily life, including the "tools for thought": *So far as I know, Up to a point, To me, the What, When, and Where indices.* (3) I saw knowledge as an abstraction, no longer a holy grail.

I built a physical model of Korzybski's structural differential to remind me of the many levels of abstracting. Some time passed before I gained a broader understanding of the phrase *the map is not the territory*. At first, I visualized geographical maps, later verbal maps (words), eventually maps of the silent level (mental pictures, abstract notions, stereotypes, vague idealizations, values, fears, hopes, etc.).

My conclusions resulted in some liberation from an oppressive set of rules about reality. Released from the *is of identity*, I no longer had to *be* anything: writer, husband, etc. I could apprehend and experience life as process, not a series of oughts and shoulds. The Aristotelian logic of polar opposites, thinking in terms of *right-wrong*, and seeking the *right* answer, had forced me into one logical dilemma after another. The vocabulary of an ongoing process improved my understanding of behavior and experience. My "failures" had arisen from inadequate tools for thought. Non-Aristotelian logic gave me more effective tools.

Although I have only begun seriously studying general semantics, I think I have learned useful methods for dealing with some practical problems of daily life. For example, I can often avoid signal reactions — those immediate responses and snap judgments in which one reacts like a "bull to a red flag" and therefore accept events more calmly, with less argument. I get angry far less than in the past, as I try to remain aware that the abstractions of others have a validity of their own. I find it easier to make decisions because I can to a greater degree separate values and assumptions from "facts." I often see that apparently conflicting situations only seem that way because of conflicting abstractions. Reviewing the abstractions in view of the overall experience often resolves the conflict. One may view "mistakes" as feedback, which redefines knowledge. Self-reflexive knowledge changes, grows, evolves.

As I endeavor to put general semantics theory into practice in daily life, I often find myself rudely reminded of the difficulties involved in breaking lifetime evaluational habits. I do not see general semantics as a panacea; certain experiences remain beyond its scope.

Nevertheless, I expect my new tools to continue to make my life more interesting and harmonious, with increasing freedom from the frozen universe of fixed states.

REFERENCES

1. E.R. Emmett, *Learning to Philosophize* (London, Longmans 1964; Pelican Books, 1968, reprinted 1969).
2. E.W. Kellogg III, Speaking in E-Prime, *Et cetera* 44, no. 2 (Summer 1987) 118-128.
3. Kenneth S. Keyes, Jr., *How to Develop Your Thinking Ability* (New York, McGraw Hill Book Company, Ltd.) 1950 & 1979.

FOR FURTHER READING

ABSOLUTISMS

Alan Walker Read, Language Revision by Deletion of Absolutisms, *Et cetera* 42, no. 1 (Spring 1985) 7-12.

E-PRIME

D. David Bourland, Jr., A Linguistic Note: Writing in E-Prime, *General Semantics Bulletin*, Institute of General Semantics, Vol. 32-33 (1965/66) 111-114.

D. David Bourland, Jr., The Semantics of a Non-Aristotelian Language, *General Semantics Bulletin*, Vol. 35 (1968) 60-63.

D. David Bourland, Jr., and Paul Dennithorne Johnston (Eds.), *To Be or Not: An E-Prime Anthology*, International Society for General Semantics, now in Concord, California, 1991.

J. Samuel Bois, *The Art of Awareness* (Dubuque, IA, Wm. C. Brown Co. Inc., 1966) 292-293.

Elaine C. Johnson, Discovering E-Prime, *Et cetera* 45, no. 2 (Summer 1988) 181-183.

Paul Dennithorne Johnston, D. David Bourland, Jr., and Jeremy Klein (Eds.), *More E-Prime: To Be or Not II*, International Society for General Semantics, Concord, California, 1994.

From *Et cetera* 46, no. 2 (Summer 1989) pages 136-140.

The Three Milk Cartons

by Robert Wanderer

I SEE THE CENTRAL POINT of general semantics as that we each continually create our own reality — by selecting perceptions from Out There and combining them with material from In Here we think is related. A nice intellectual point, but how can it be illustrated physically?

The three milk cartons demonstrate this.

Take three empty milk cartons: a half-gallon, a pint and a half-pint. Add a little sand or other weighty material (the same material in each carton) so that the two larger cartons each weigh 16 ounces and the smallest carton weighs 12 ounces. Then seal the cartons and, if you wish, paint them different colors.

The question is: Which weighs the most? There are seven possible answers: each of the three cartons, the three combinations of two equally heavy cartons, or all three weigh the same.

Have your students come up and examine the cartons any way they wish. When everyone is finished, take a vote on the seven possibilities.

Opinions are usually quite mixed. The middle-sized carton may get the most votes, with the small one coming in second, and the two smaller ones being equally scored next, perhaps followed by all three being equal.

Then produce a small postal or other scale and ask someone to weigh the cartons.

The correct answer, that the two larger cartons are equally heavy and the smaller carton lighter, invariably stuns everyone. In 20 years of using this demonstration, I can recall only one instance of anyone selecting the correct answer, and he was an immigrant from a quite different culture (Polynesian, I think).

Why does everyone miss? Some people are so annoyed by the answer that they develop theories of how my instructions were unfair, or of the alleged psychological effect of the colors with which the cartons were painted. It's usually a lively discussion.

The key point is that we all have learned — indeed, we taught ourselves very early in life that big things usually weigh more than little things. Therefore when we prepare to lift something large we "automatically" apply more muscle tension to lift it. So while we think we are comparing the weights of the cartons, we are actually comparing our experiences with the cartons. And these experiences are our combination of the actual carton Out There and our way of abstracting the weight of that carton and of employing the "proper" muscle tension we think is called for In Here.

Some students may want to try experiencing the cartons further. Let a student come forward, hold hands out flat and close eyes, and then you randomly place cartons on the hands. The larger area of the bottom of the larger cartons and the feeling of the balance of the cartons will tend to bring about the same mistake. Or have the student close eyes and hold fingers-and-thumbs out for grasping the cartons, and the feeling of the variation of swinging motion related to the length of the cartons will continue the problem.

Or, instead of cartons, use three medicine-size bottles of similar varying sizes and weights as before.

(Source: I got this from the late Norman Harrington, who taught general semantics at San Quentin Prison for many years.)

From *Et cetera* 44, no. 2 (Summer 1987) pages 190-191.

Was it Kierkegaard or Dick Van Patten who said, "If you label me, you negate me"?

From *Wayne's World,* the movie (1992)

The Nine-Dot Problem

by Robert Wanderer

I CONSIDER THE NINE-DOT PROBLEM the best single demonstration of how we misinterpret "reality." Many people have seen this exercise before in books and articles on creative thinking. But the assumptions involved are so strong that I find that even those people often forget how to solve it.

Put the nine dots on the blackboard, or on sheets of paper, as shown here. The instructions are to connect all nine dots with four straight lines that run continuously; in other words, draw them without taking your pencil off the paper, with the second line starting at the end of the first, the third at the end of the second, and the fourth at the end of the third.

I present this nine-dot problem in the first class of every course I teach, and it's extremely rare that anyone who hasn't seen it before is able to solve it. And many of those who have seen it before may have a vague idea of the solution, but can't get it quite right. I ask those who do remember the answer not to tell it, while the rest of the group stews over what some of them come to regard as an impossible problem.

Allow plenty of time for them to work — long enough so they will appreciate the lesson all the more, but not long enough for boredom and frustration to set in. I sometimes "help" by mentioning that there are actually 16 ways of solving the problem, and that I will accept any one of them. When they groan and ask for more useful "help," I point out that the difficulty lies with what they are assuming. That ordinarily is no help whatsoever, since the assumptions are so strong that we are not aware we are making any.

Finally, the solution: Start, say, at the upper dot of the left column. Draw the first line to the right through the upper row of dots and on one "space" to the right of the right column. The second line goes "southwest" from there through the middle dot of the right column and the bottom dot of the middle column to a point one "space" below the bottom dot of the first column. The third line goes up through the dots of the left column to the starting point. The fourth line goes "southeast" through the center dot of the middle column and the bottom dot of the right column.

Virtually everyone experiences two problems here:

1. We tend to regard the dots as a "box" or boundary.
2. We tend to make up the rule that the lines cannot go "beyond the box."

Beautiful. We create our problem by seeing what we think "ought" to be there, and then limit ourselves further by creating another restriction.

People who have seen this before usually remember that they have to go "beyond the dots," but often they can't remember just how. There seem to be some further assumptions here: I suspect we resist recall because the result somehow looks "unbalanced," the place where the lines cross is somehow not where it "should" be, and that second line somehow doesn't seem "logical."

As for the 16 solutions: the one I outlined here on page 77 can be drawn four ways, starting at either "end" and turning in either direction, and the similar four can be done from each of the four "corners."

From *Et cetera* 44, no. 1 (Spring 1987) pages 86-87.

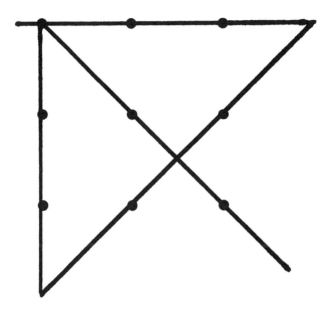

ONE SOLUTION TO THE NINE-DOT PROBLEM

Maps on First

by Andrea Johnson

I KNOW MANY GENERAL SEMANTICISTS will tell you that we live in a world of processes and we cannot pinpoint finite beginnings and endings. And ordinarily I agree. Yet every semester I face a room full of open faces and I control the inauguration — what do I teach first? In the beginning there is "the map."

By the end of the first class, my students have faithfully learned Korzybski's analogy. I must admit that I do find something reassuring in the choral-like way they chant the first refrain, "the map is not the territory," followed by the resplendent peal, "the word is not the thing." Unfortunately, this parroting does not reflect an understanding of the principle. And so, for the second class session, I have developed an exercise to act as a bridge between "the map" and the students' territories.

In one of Sawin's *Et cetera* columns, he stated that each of us was born into a culture of beliefs, customs, and a language that shaped our mental maps. (1) He further asserted that

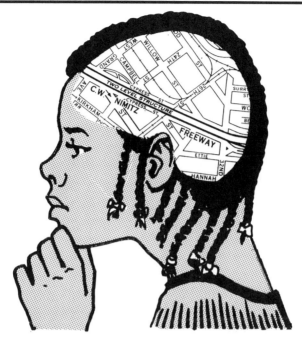

parents and teachers encouraged us to adopt these prefabricated mental maps. Using his words as a stimulus, I lead students through a simple activity which helps them articulate their cultural maps, identify the origins of these maps, and then evaluate their usefulness and timeliness.

Each student completes the following eight sentence fragments:

- Good girls...
- People who...
- Don't ever...
- A good student...

- Everyone will like you if...
- Only lazy people...
- A successful man...
- You can always tell a...by...

After they've completed the sentences, I ask them to review what they've written to see if they can (1) identify where their maps came from (Who may have said or suggested these words?), (2) determine the usefulness of their maps (How have the maps helped shape or guide their attitudes, their behaviors?), and (3) find a fit between their prefabricated maps and their correct territories (Do their maps need updating? Tossing?).

At this point, the students eagerly share their sentences and their analyses with each other. Naturally, there's some silly stuff (don't ever pick your nose in public), some platitudes (people who live in glass houses...), and then some painfully honest disclosures (you can always tell a lesbian by...).

Together we re-examine Sawin's ideas in connection with the statements they've just produced. The students literally straighten up as they begin to get it.

"These are maps."

"These are my mother's maps (or Rev. Brown's, or my third grade teacher's, or my brother's, or my Auntie's maps). Are they mine too?"

"Can I change the map? Will it change my attitude? Will it fit the territory?"

These kinds of questions provide fertile ground for further exchanges about maps, territories, perceptions, abstractions, inferences, judgments, and so on.

From time to time I still encourage my students to break into a rousing chorus of "the map...." I like to hear that old familiar tune. But it's never quite like the first time. While the words remain the same, the melody seems different. Because now they've played this song through the instruments of their own experiences. The first map is not the second, is not the third, is not...

REFERENCE

1. G. Sawin, How Could I Be Wrong About Her?, *Et cetera* 46, no. 4 (Winter 1989) 375-377; also appears in this book.

From *Et cetera* 49, no. 1 (Spring 1992) pages 86-88.

Writing to Real People

by Andrea Johnson

E ssay? Research paper? Editorial? Response paper? For eight semesters, I've taught an introductory course in general semantics at Alverno College, Milwaukee. And for eight semesters, I've searched for a powerful end-of-the-course writing assignment that would enable students to integrate general semantics principles with personal awarenesses. This phantom assignment would reach into their nervous systems and help them (1) evaluate personal experiences; (2) recognize changes in behaviors and attitudes; and (3) apply general semantics formulations to 1 and 2.

My previous attempts at creating a comprehensive assignment had met with various degrees of success. Even when students gave me lovingly written papers that could attest to their understanding of general semantics, I felt as if something was missing. I couldn't hear their voices — the perimeters of past papers seemed too confining and the students' words seemed constricted.

This semester I tried a new approach. I told my students about two friends I had met at the 1989 General Semantics Summer Seminar-Workshop, Dominique Benoit and Pascale de la Saussay. They intend to organize an Institute of General Semantics in France. I suggested that Dominique and Pascale would enjoy hearing from students who could share ideas about how they applied general semantics to their personal or professional situations.

At first the students gasped. "You want us to write to real people who will really read this?!" Recovering from the ego-diminishing discovery that I wasn't real, I assured them that they had grasped the concept. They responded with suspicion — "Will you correct the letters, have us rewrite and then send them out?" No. Each student makes two copies of the letter; one gets mailed and one gets assessed. "I suppose you'll send only the best letters." No, again. Each letter will be forwarded. Armed with a one-page outline of the assignment, the students accepted the challenge and began their work.

I didn't need to read all seventy letters before I knew I had something special in my hands. The lump in my throat told me that. The students' responses reflected the diversity of their backgrounds, ages, situations, and understanding of general semantics formulations. One thing remained constant, however: they saw real connections between their lives and what they had learned over the semester. With the permission of my students, I'd like to share samples of their work.

The Sibling Connection (Several students chose to focus on how to improve a tenuous relationship with their brothers or sisters.) "When I was beginning to understand the notion of *dating*, I found it easier to talk with my sister. Every time we talked, I tried to remember that she was different from the time before. Sure, we still argue, but it is a lot easier to talk with her an hour after an argument because I know I will be somewhat different than we were while arguing. I don't think that general semantics will make any of my relationships problem-free, but understanding the dating notion will continue to help me work out problems over time."

Self-Image Observations (Many students used this letter to articulate how they now viewed themselves and to specu-

late on how they thought others viewed them.) "As a child, I was told I wasn't pretty enough to have boyfriends, or athletic enough to participate in sports, or talented enough to play the piano. For years I carried these maps with me, accepting them, as only an innocent child can, to be true. My general semantics class has helped me to better understand the constraints placed upon me by other people's ideals. The three principles that gave me the greatest insights are 'the map is not the territory,' indexing, and abstractions."

"Labels keep people apart by blinding them to any other aspect of the person. I encounter this type of labeling quite frequently because I am overweight. When people look at me they usually don't see an articulate, intelligent, well-mannered student of general semantics; they see a fat person. Because this label is painful to accept, I tend to become defensive and I retreat. Because I now realize a little better why people react the way they do, I am less defensive and so I can help others realize that fat person 1 is not fat person 2."

"The principles of general semantics have taught me that many of the difficulties I experienced with my self-worth came about because I confused 'me' with my roles. My roles will continue to change, yet the 'me' in me will still remain. I can now work toward enhancing my inner self, and I can go out into the community and the world around me without feeling restricted by my role labels."

Relationship Conflicts (A recurring theme: girl meets boy, girl gets boy, girl reevaluates boy, girl wises up.) "As I learned more about general semantics, I saw some of the mistakes I was making in my relationships. It occurred to me that both of us had very different ideas about love and commitment. I realized my map needed to be updated. I was cheating myself out of new experiences because my old map had me deadlocked. General semantics didn't save this relationship, but it did give me a clearer understanding about myself. It also gave me some useful tools to employ in future relationships. General semantics gave me some answers to some questions and freed me from my life in an intensional* world."

Cross-Cultural Understanding (A Japanese exchange student provided me with a new appreciation for second-language learners.) "English is my second language, and American culture was unfamiliar to me when I first came to America. Sometimes people tried hard to understand me,

---

* Editor's note: "Intensional" means knowledge based on words, rather than knowledge based on observed facts.

and sometimes they thought they understood when they did not. As time passed, my English skills improved, but there came new problems. Some people saw me as a Japanese, but not as an individual. Those people put their stereotypes of all Japanese on me. This bothered me a lot until I understand some of the reasons for stereotyping. I suspect that it was easy for people to stereotype me because I was not able to communicate enough to show my individuality. Soon I became able to think in English and deliver English words more smoothly. People could then index that Japanese 1 is not Japanese 2, but then a new problem started. I began to feel two personalities in me — one when I spoke Japanese and one when I spoke English. I pondered this a lot and wondered if I had a psychological problem. Now I understand that the differences in languages had an effect on me. When I speak in English, I can say things more clearly and directly so that I feel myself as a direct person. However, when I speak in Japanese, I have to select from so many ways to say one thing that I have to choose carefully. Each way has a slightly different connotation, so that automatically I am more careful and thus more indirect and shy. By applying the principles of general semantics to my second-language learning process in America, I can see what happened to me both inside and out."

The World of Work (Most of my students depend upon outside employment to pay for their college education. Several letters looked at their work environ-

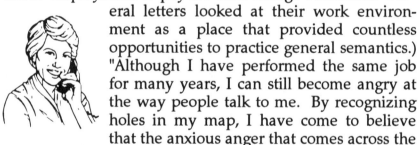

ment as a place that provided countless opportunities to practice general semantics.) "Although I have performed the same job for many years, I can still become angry at the way people talk to me. By recognizing holes in my map, I have come to believe that the anxious anger that comes across the phone lines is not being directed at me personally. I then feel more compelled to help this person out rather than return the anger I hear in their voices. By updating my map, dating and indexing customers, and knowing that there is an 'etc.' in every situation, I have become a more effective communicator at work."

Dealing with Domestic Violence (Even after working closely with students for four months, I could not imagine some of the pain they managed to work through in my class.) "The violent behavior I tolerated during the marriage took a toll on my self-esteem, self-image, and self-concept. Through the general semantics principles of dating, indexing, and the-map-is-not-the-territory, I repossessed some measure of self-trust and confidence. The idea of self 'then' and self 'here-now' is critical in helping me focus on an idea/task/issue without discounting what learning has occurred between failure-in-past and today's goals. I allow a range of problem-solving skills to gain strength which over time, with each success, builds confidence to use those skills toward more successes. After  the violence experience in marriage, I struggle to maintain that man 1 is not man 2 is not man 3. Even though I know that not all men are violent, I am terrified of anger. As long as I can see that anger 1 is not anger 2 is not anger 3, I remain calm and safe. This principle helps prevent generalizations about what I fear, which in turn allows me to see the world more accurately. What started as 'stupid about' soon shifted to 'too stupid to...' and on toward feeling hopeless. This was perhaps the most critical factor in shattering my self-esteem and confidence. By understanding that I had created maps about my maps of my example's maps, I recognized the need to lay aside those maps and examine the territory. I found this crucial in reestablishing a healthy relationship with myself."

Testimonials (They speak for themselves.) "Studying two-valued orientation has helped me see the gray areas in life.

This idea of gray areas helped me in a group project. In this course we were expected to discuss a controversial issue within our group. My group argued for days over who was 'right' and who was 'wrong.' Finally, I realized what we were facing. I brought in my general semantics text and explained two-valued orientation to the rest of my group members. After that, we were able to focus on the 'gray' areas of the issue."

"With reinforcement from my general semantics class, I now try harder than ever to avoid absolutes such as 'always' and 'never' in my speech; I try not to lump people into categories; and I try to balance 'facts' that might otherwise have me thinking in extremes."

"In the past, the only conditions I could see involved choices between good and bad, right and wrong, black and white. I will forever be grateful to Andrea for helping me discover that the world actually comes in assorted shades of gray."

It seems to me that looking for the "perfect" writing assignment is antithetical to the principles of general semantics. However, as educators, we can look for and find ways for students to participate at their own levels of comprehension and application. We can give them a voice. Perhaps this means writing to real people about real happenings in their lives. (And the papers are in the mail!)

From *Et cetera* 47, no. 2 (Summer 1990) pages 188-192.

Statement of Fact or Statement of Inference *

by Ruth Gonchar Brennan

I WAS ENROLLED 25 years ago, fall semester, in a speech course entitled "General Semantics." Harry Weinberg was the teacher. On one particular day, he was trying to bang into the heads of his general semantics students distinctions between the concepts of *fact* and *inference*. We were an intransigent class.

Toward the end of the class, Dr. Weinberg offered us some statements and we were asked to determine whether they were statements of fact or inference. Harry Weinberg offered us the following example: "Fact or inference," he said, "John F. Kennedy is President of the United States." "Fact," we shouted in unison. "Fact?" he responded. "We've all been in class for almost an hour. Who's to say as a matter of fact that John Kennedy is President of the United States? It is an *infer-*

---

* Reprinted with permission from the Winter 1988-1989 issue of *The Temple Review*, Temple University, Philadelphia, PA 19122.

What is a fact?

ence, although it's a highly probable one. He might have re-signed, his back pain may have incapacitated him, he might even have been killed. Such a statement is *not* one of fact."

Class was over and I started to walk across campus. It was just slightly after noon on November 22, 1963. A young woman sat on the ground with tears streaming down her face. "Someone shot the President," she said. "Which President?" I asked. "Our President," she cried.

I will always remember that day. On November 22, 1963, I began mourning a dead President. I miss him still.

Several years later, Harry Weinberg died, not violently like Kennedy, but peacefully. I mourned his passing as well. I miss him still.

From *Et cetera* 46, no. 2 (Summer 1989) page 141.

An Exercise
in Reporting

by Ruth McCubbrey

F OR THE PAST week and a half in Critical Thinking (the now name the Board of Education came up with for the senior English course I previously called "General Semantics") we've been studying the differences between *reports* (a report is capable of verification and excludes inferences and judgments), *inferences* (statements about the unknown based on the known), and *judgments* (all expressions of the writer's approval or disapproval of the occurrences, persons, or objects he is describing — what Hayakawa calls "snarls" and "purrs"). After taking the Haney "Uncritical Inference Test," reading Hayakawa's "Reports, Inferences and Judgments" from *Language in Thought and Action* and observing the way *Time Magazine* snarls and purrs as it delivers its "unbiased" news, students seem quite able to distinguish genuine reports from those colored by inferences and judgments. They can, for instance, label the following examples:

I saw Dick and Jane walking across campus holding hands [REPORT]. They must be going together [INFERENCE].

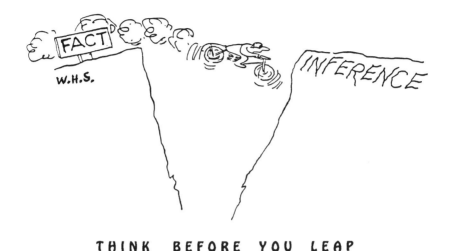

THINK BEFORE YOU LEAP

Can't imagine why Jane is going with Dick — He's such a dork [JUDGMENT].

Student studying report card: I got an F in U.S. History?? [REPORT]. Boy, Mr. Potter really has it in for me [INFERENCE]. He's a real S.O.B. [JUDGMENT].

Student Analysis of Magazine Ads

Today students have brought in magazine ads and will be telling the class what *facts* are in each and what *inferences* one might make from reading the ad copy and viewing the illustrations.

For example, a young man telling about a Pierre Cardin ad says, "the facts are that it is a cologne made for men and that the accessories in the picture are courtesy of Tiffany and Co. Yeah. Tiffany. See the solid gold cufflinks, the gold watch, the gold lighter? — even the keys look like they're made of solid gold! Note the words at the top of the ad: 'The fragrance the well-dressed tycoon is wearing.' You get the idea: wear this stuff, man, and you'll feel rich, classy — you'll be wearing what the most powerful men in America wear. You may even pick yourself up some great accessories from Tiffany. And finally! Notice the shape of the bottle...reminds you of an erect penis, right? Not only will you feel rich, you'll be a potent stud!"

A young woman has an ad for Salem cigarettes: "The facts in the ad are that there are 10 mg. tar and 0.8 mg. nicotine in the average cigarette and the surgeon general warns that cigarette smoking is dangerous to your health. Now: look at those great-looking guys and gals playing touch football in the snow. They're having a terrific time! See them laugh as they put their hands all over each other. The words, 'You've got what it takes. Salem Spirit', don't mean a thing — but I infer that if I smoke Salem, I've got spirit and I'll have some good times with my good-looking friends. You might also notice how clean and fresh the environment looks in the picture. Probably because no one is smoking..."

Six students have discussed their ads before I call on Joe, a young man who usually attends class but rarely does his homework. Joe is hunched over his desk, flipping noisily through a magazine.

"Joe?" [Silence.]

"Joe — you're up next."

"I don't have it," Joe states emphatically, glowering down at the magazine in his hands.

"Why not?"

"I. Just. Don't." [Hostile glare in my direction.]

"Joe...remember the talk we had with your father..."

"You stupid bitch!" Joe explodes, his face turning a mottled red — and he storms out of the classroom, slamming the door so hard the windows rattle.

I am shaking as I hand out sheets of paper to the stunned class members. "Please write a report of what just happened," I ask. Some frown, others shift uncomfortably in their seats, but all start to write.

Ten minutes later I collect the "reports." Then, going to the door, I open it and Joe, grinning wickedly at the baffled expressions on the students' faces, enters and swaggers nonchalantly to his seat. The class hadn't realized that I'd seen Joe on my way to the faculty mailroom that morning and that we'd set the whole thing up. Well...almost the whole thing. The language was Joe's.

["Joe?" I'd said.
"I'll have an absence slip for yesterday," Joe responded. "It was *excused*."
"Interesting inference," I'd commented drily before asking for his help: "When I call on you today for your ad assignment, I'd like you to say you're not prepared."
"No problem there — I didn't do it." After a brief discussion in which I assured Joe he'd get credit for the assignment, Joe agreed to the setup and departed, eyes sparkling.]

Reports or Inferences?

"So!" I say to the bemused students, "What were your inferences? Why did you think I asked you to write these reports?" Most, it turns out, assumed I would turn the reports over to the principal when I asked him to remove Joe permanently from the class. [I hadn't counted on that. Did I feel chagrined!]

"Okay, let's look at these reports, class." I read each aloud. The first reads,

The teacher called on Joe to do his ad assignment. Typically, Joe was unprepared — probably out partying last night, as usual. (Joe holds the school record for most beers consumed in one evening.) Teach said something about a talk with Joe's dad which was really kneeing him in the groin. Everyone knows Joe and his dad don't get along — his dad is always ragging on him. So naturally Joe got mad and left.

"Is this a genuine report?" I ask. "Did anyone spot any inferences? Any judgments about either Joe or me?" The class members laugh and I see dawning comprehension. "Probably out partying" one calls out. "Kneeing in the groin"..."everyone knows"..."naturally Joe got mad."

"Good! Let's look at another one."

Ms. McCubbrey asked Joe to give his ad. "I'm not ready," Joe told her in an angry tone of voice. Ms. McC sweetly asked why not. Joe got even madder. She gently said something about his father and Joe called her an awful name and left, slamming the door. You treat him so nice, Ms. McCubbrey. Don't feel bad. He's just as awful in other classes.

By the end of the reading of reports — few of which, it turns out, are straight reports — and discussion, students seem to understand how difficult it is to keep reports from being colored by inferences and judgments. They resolve to be better report writers in the future.

●   ●   ●

For those worried about Joe's reaction to the "reports": He laughed loudly and repeatedly throughout the reading and discussion. In the following weeks he began doing much of the homework, finally passing the class with a C+, the highest grade he received for any class that semester.

Eventually Joe went on to get a degree in psychology from San Francisco State University.

From *Et cetera* 44, no. 2 (Summer 1987) pages 187-189.

On Consciousness of Abstracting or Let's Party!

by Ruth McCubbrey

Thirty-five high school seniors, all with self-sticking labels on their foreheads, are looking up at me expectantly. "Anyone want to party?" I ask. Several grin and nod, others look at one another with their "she's-at-it-again" expressions, while a few call out "bitchin'!" and "go for it!"

As a teacher of general semantics in a public high school for fifteen years, I have developed ways of demonstrating some general semantics formulations which help my students understand and appreciate more fully the topic we are studying. If the students can get a "feeling in their guts" first, they seem more willing to do the spade work necessary for an intellectual understanding. And class discussions tend to be far more lively and involved.

Before class started on this day, I had made out the labels, each of which had on it a different role designation: school group, occupation, age, or economic group. Cautioning students not to divulge each other's labels, I stuck one to each forehead.

W. H. Schneider cartoon adapted by G. Sawin
W.H.S.

"Okay," I continue, "let's pretend we're at a party. As you walk around and talk with the other people in the classroom, react to them as you would if they actually were what their labels state. The object is to discover what label you are wearing through the clues given by other class members."

Some Effects of Labeling

As I walk about the classroom, I hear students giving each other rather broad hints. [To *truck driver*: "Do you have problems with hemorrhoids?" To *pimp*: "Hey! I know someone you'd like to meet" as he leads him over to the *hooker*. To *policeman*: "Get a thrill out of busting teenagers?" To *lawyer*: "Been chasing many ambulances lately?" To *stoner*: "How many brain cells you figure you got left?"] Thus the game ends fairly quickly (usually five to ten minutes) — which is all to the good since my *real* object is to discuss what happens when we see another person as being just one "thing."

99

I begin the discussion with a specific question: What did you talk about with the *six-year-old*? [Most asked how she liked school, what grade she was in; the *six-year-old* reported angrily that she felt patronized. And students became aware that when they speak to children, they alter their tone of voice.] Then students begin to chime in with, "*You* felt patronized?! I was a *cheerleader* and everyone acted like I was a complete airhead." "Oh yeah?" another retorts. "I was a *freshman* and almost everyone told me to get lost, dipshit." "That's nothing," a husky young man says. "I was a *ballet dancer*, and although a few asked questions about how high I could leap, most made 'cutesy' remarks about how adorable I must look in my pink tutu and said in mincing voices, 'I bet you just l-o-v-e being with other fellas.'"

"Didn't anyone have a positive experience?" I ask. Dead silence. Then: "Well, at least the few people who spoke to me treated me with respect," the *nun* reports. "But most just said 'Uh-oh — I'd better watch my language.' — and then took off. I figured I must be an English teacher." [Big laugh from class here.] The *surgeon* agrees that he felt respected — even though one asked him if he'd ever left any sponges or tools inside a patient — and the *airline pilot* reports that people did seem interested in his job, asking him what countries he'd been to and if he'd ever been hijacked.

"Were any of you aware of changing your manner of speaking according to what the label represented?" I see some nods, and one student says slowly, "You know, I realized that I felt somewhat intimidated by the *multimillionaire*: somehow I felt she would think I was 'beneath' her, so I spoke rather deferentially." "Hey! Yeah!" another says — "and I remember talking especially loudly to the *89-year-old* and putting my arm around his shoulders." "And you called me 'gramps' you jerk." [Dirty look.] The *housewife* reports that people seemed to be smirking at her while they asked about the kind of bleach she thinks works best, what soap operas she watches regularly, and what her husband's job was.

"Why do you think people would ask what your husband's job was?" She doesn't know — but gradually students reach an understanding that one's status is usually job-related. A housewife's status, then, would be different depending upon her husband's job; i.e., a *senator's* wife would have higher status than a *garbage collector's* wife.

Who Am I?

Before bringing the discussion to a close, I ask my students to get out a sheet of paper and write at the top WHO AM I? I give them ten minutes to fill up the sheet with nouns which describe them. [I immediately begin writing my own list on the board to help them get started: teacher, mother, runner, skier, pianist, feminist, twin, ice cream junkie, dog owner, Bill Cosby fan, risk-taker, opera-lover, Democrat, travel-lover, general semanticist, etc.]

"What if someone treated you as though ALL you were was just one item on your list? Has anyone been seen as 'just' a teenager? a 'jock'? a skateboarder? a computer 'freak'? a 'scammer'? a blonde? a bookworm? a surfer? How did it make you feel?"

Stereotypes

By the end of the period, students seem fully aware that in the Party Game they were relating to one another on the basis of only one characteristic and that had made them treat people as the stereotypes they had of those roles. Too, they understand that this kind of thing happens a lot in real life. [For example, one male student reported, "If I'd known you were a *feminist*, I'd have checked out of this class the first day."] Finally, they see that — just as each of them is composed of a multiplicity of characteristics, qualities, interests, values, etc. — so, too, is everyone else in the world.

My students are starting to become conscious of their own abstracting processes and to see how important this awareness is in the avoidance of stereotyping.

From *Et cetera* 43, no. 4 (Winter 1986) pages 410-412.

Oh To Be a Writer

by Andrea Johnson

"In order to write factually, you have to tell it like it is."

*"If a thought is about you, and it is
written by you, then you write: 'I am.'"*

S O RESPOND my students when asked to identify helpful
writing paradigms. After listing these handy homilies,
they confidently move to review their next writing assignment: a one-page autobiography. Several brows furrow, and
one student asks, "What do you mean, 'write this paper in
E-Prime'?" "Ahh," I reply. "Good question."

E-Prime

Dr. Kenneth G. Johnson introduced me to E-Prime, the
writings of D. David Bourland, Jr., and not coincidentally the
E-Prime autobiography assignment, when I studied general
semantics as a graduate student at the University of Wis-

consin-Milwaukee. Bourland, a student of Korzybski, coined the term E-Prime to signify English minus the verb "to be" — *is, am, are, were, was, be, being, been.* Bourland suggests that writing and speaking without using any forms of the verb "to be" can assist the user in attaining a kind of vigorous clarity. More importantly, he notes that E-Prime functions as an additional extensional device as it provides a means for making more accurate mappings.

I offer this background information to my students, along with a copy of Bourland's article, "To Be or Not To Be: E-Prime as a Tool for Critical Thinking." (1) Now, disarmed of their writing caveats and looking decidedly concerned, they take their assignments home.

The following week, before discussing their work, I ask the students to evaluate the exercise and then write their responses to the assignment.

1. Relate your experience in writing your autobiography in E-Prime. What proved most difficult? Easiest?
2. Bourland suggests that writing in E-Prime keeps you honest because you focus on the territory (what you *do*) rather than the map (what you *say* you are). After writing this autobiography, what do you think?
3. What if you could have used *to be* verbs in this exercise. Would the picture of you seem different if you had said "I am" or "I was"?
4. Will you use E-Prime in the future?

What the Students Learned by Using E-Prime

And what did they think, feel, believe, sense, learn, identify, observe?

"It forced me to pay more attention to what I wanted to say. It's easy to say 'I am a mother,' but what does that really mean?"

"I might develop my work more if I had to fully explain myself. I know I should do this anyway, but if I write in E-Prime, I couldn't get around it."

"E-Prime forces you to follow some of the rules of general semantics — you become more conscious of maps and your extensional world."

"After writing this paper, I think of myself as having more confidence and strength. I made a clearer map of me and how I see the territory. I feel like I learned a lot about myself."

"The most difficult part was getting out of the habit of labeling myself as 'being' something. If I can eliminate some labeling, it will be easier for a reader to understand what I mean."

"Without E-Prime, I would have made more absolute statements about what are essentially self-perceptions."

"Even while writing this response, I've noticed how many times I've used 'to be' — it gets annoying."

"I don't think I would have sounded as creative if I had used 'to be' verbs. 'To be' verbs do not really describe anything accurately or interestingly. This assignment has made me more aware of how often I use 'to be' and the effect it has on my writing. I will try to cut down."

At the end of the semester, when asked to evaluate the most helpful or valuable assignments in class, many students named the E-Prime autobiography. Several noticed that they had learned how to talk more positively about themselves. Some suggested that using E-Prime helped clarify the meanings of intensional and extensional orientations for them.* Others observed an improvement in their ability to write from a clearer analytical perspective.

One student said she liked the E-Prime exercise best because she had always wanted to be a writer and now, she happily proclaimed, "I am a writer!". A student who knew how to listen in E-Prime tactfully advised, "Maryanne, you probably learned how to write better." Yep.

NOTE AND REFERENCE

1. D.D. Bourland, Jr., To Be or Not To Be: E-Prime as a Tool for Critical Thinking, *Et cetera* 46, no. 3 (Fall 1989). It also appears in *To Be or Not: An E-Prime Anthology*, edited by D. David Bourland, Jr. & Paul Dennithorne Johnston. In slightly expanded form it appears as a chapter in K.G. Johnson's *Thinking Creatically*. Both books are available from the International Society for General Semantics.

*Editor's note: "Intensional" means based on words; "extensional" means based on observations.

From *Et cetera* 49, no. 2 (Summer 1992) pages 168-170.

Do Away with "To Be" — There, Pupils, Lies the Answer *

by E. W. Kellogg III

D OES THE ENGLISH LANGUAGE really need the verb *to be* or does its use involve more liabilities than benefits? For the past several hundred years, philosophers, scholars, and English teachers have warned against the abuse of the verb (basically *am, are, is, was, were, be* and *been*).

More pragmatically, English teachers continue to tell students: "Vary your verb choices! Use the active voice! Release trapped verbs! Say who did what to whom!" These pretty much boil down to one simple rule: "Avoid the verb *to be*!" But in the past even those who warned against the verb continued using it themselves.

E-Prime

In 1965, D. David Bourland, Jr., now a retired professor of linguistics, made the audacious suggestion that we could give up the use of *to be* altogether, and that this modification

of English (labeled by him "English-Prime" or "E-Prime") might even improve the language. At first, Bourland's idea may sound odd and impractical, but over the past 25 years numerous articles, books, and even dissertations have confirmed E-Prime's usefulness.

Some advocates consider E-Prime a more descriptive form of English that tends to bring the user back to the "level of first-person experience." It eliminates the over-defining of situations that confuse one aspect of an experience with a much more complex totality. This occurs mainly in sentences using the "is of identity" ("John *is* a jerk") and the "is of predication" ("The apple *is* red"). Writing can improve with E-Prime because users must often replace the passive voice ("It was done") with the more informative active voice ("Russell did it"). It also encourages the use of verbs other than *to be* by eliminating sentence structures of the X *is* Y form ("Elaine *is* a teacher") and using subject-verb-object structures instead ("Elaine teaches English").

The verb *to be* encourages the "Deity mode" of speech, as seen frequently in political speeches and in statements such as "This is the truth." Even the most uninformed can use this  mode to transform their opinions magically into godlike pronouncements on the objective nature of things. E-Prime minimizes such presumption, and users must often take overt responsibility for their opinions. For example, "The Northlight is a good restaurant" might become "I enjoy eating at the Northlight restaurant." The unrecognized assumptions that *to be* often introduces can also impair perceptivity and even creativity. For example, compare "The man is drunk" to "The man acts drunk" or "There is no solution to this problem" to "No one has solved this problem yet."

Does E-Prime have any disadvantages? Well, practitioners lose *to be* as an auxiliary verb, to indicate existence and to create metaphors. Although some critics would say that such losses reduce the viability of E-Prime as an independent language, most at least appreciate its effectiveness in the short term as a pedagogic tool. So far, some English teachers have established that courses in E-Prime can provide a practical and entertaining way of helping students gain awareness of how they overuse and abuse the verb *to be*, and of the opportunities offered by other verb choices and sentence structures.

Limitations of E-Prime

E-Prime involves a number of limitations that many would find onerous, and one would no more expect it to appeal to the majority of English-speaking people than a low-fat vegetarian diet would to the same group. The controversy over E-Prime has just begun, and the summer [1992] issue of *ETC: A Review of General Semantics* presents many of the pros and cons of the issue. Although practitioners of E-Prime advocate the complete elimination of *to be*, they assert than any reduction in the use of the verb can have beneficial effects. The future success of the movement for such reduction may not depend upon its wide acceptance, but upon its adoption by individuals who use it because of its practical value.

DeWitt Scott, an editor for the *San Francisco Examiner*, wrote that "removing the supreme irritant, *to be*, forces me to express myself in straightforward statements and come out of the clouds." Robert Ian Scott, a professor of English at the University of Saskatchewan, minimized his use of *to be* to such an extent in his textbook *The Specific Writer* that less than five percent of the sentences use the verb. The February, 1992, issue of *The Atlantic Monthly* magazine brought the idea of E-Prime to the attention of a broad audience in an article called "'To Be' in Their Bonnets." (1)

George Santayana put it this way in *Skepticism and Animal Faith*: "Whenever I use the word *is*, except in sheer tautology, I deeply misuse it; and when I discover my error, the world seems to fall asunder and the members of my family no longer know one another."

REFERENCE

1. C. Murphy, "To Be" in Their Bonnets, *The Atlantic Monthly*, Feb. 1992, pages 18-24.

E-PRIME BOOKS

D. David Bourland, Jr., and Paul Dennithorne Johnston (Eds.), *To Be or Not: An E-Prime Anthology*, International Society for General Semantics, now in Concord, California, 1991.

Paul Dennithorne Johnston, D. David Bourland, Jr., and Jeremy Klein (Eds.), *More E-Prime: To Be or Not II*, International Society for General Semantics, Concord, California, 1994.

From *Et cetera* 50, no. 3 (Fall 1993) pages 311-313.
First published in *Newsday*, September 16, 1992.

Authority of Words: Uncertainty of Life

by Rachel M. Lauer

A N OBSOLETE STREET MAP can mislead a visitor to a city. Streets might have been re-named, re-routed, made inaccessible or even obliterated as the city changed. Language, like a map that ignores a changing reality, can make us believe in certainty that doesn't exist. However, we can take precautions against its false promises of security.

This article is derived from one seminar on Thinking & Communicating created by and for faculty at Pace University in New York. (1) Faculty meet for two hours per week. They apply the topics to their own disciplines and also prepare to teach the subject as a whole under the heading of critical thinking. Enthusiastically, they suggested our materials and procedures might be of value to groups outside the university.

The Map Is Not the Territory

In this seminar, we usually start with a concrete demonstration, followed by a discussion and practice exercises. To

Life   Words

remind a class to think of language as a map *of* something else, or as a code *for* something else, I present the riddle:

"Whatever I say something is, it is not."

If the class doesn't perceive the riddle's meaning, I underline the word "say." Whatever I *say* about something is not the same as the something itself. The map is not the territory.

If some people still miss the point, I ask the class to close their eyes. I crumple a piece of paper and ask, "What did you *hear*?" Usually someone says, "I heard a paper crumpling," to which I reply, "Did anyone hear the words 'paper crumpling'?" No one did. If they are still mystified, I take a piece of white chalk and write on the board "Green." I ask, "What color is that?" Some reply it's green, others that it is white. Most now recognize the crucial difference between the word "green" and the non-verbal experience of white. To clinch the point, I write the word "water" on the board and ask if anyone can drink it. No one can.

Two Worlds: Verbal and Non-Verbal

Thus we emphasize the easily forgotten truth of two worlds: one is the non-verbal world that we observe with our senses and various other instruments. The other is the world of symbols with which we map or codify what we observe. Although we can symbolize with numbers or pictures, more often we use language. Although we realize that words are not the things they represent, often we do not realize how poorly our verbal maps fit the territories we're talking about. During the course on thinking and communicating, we work at finding better matches between what we observe and what we say. Such efforts may be vital to accuracy, and accuracy may sometimes be vital to human welfare.

The short test below illustrates some important points.

Instructions: Below are some statements — some generalizations about what people have observed. Mark each one TRUE; or, if it is not always true, mark it FALSE.

___ 1. Apples are red.

___ 2. Milk is good for people.

___ 3. One and one make two.

___ 4. The speed of sound is 741.5 miles per hour.

___ 5. AIDS causes death.

___ 6. Reagan is a Republican.

Even some of the most sophisticated college professors will mark one or more of the above sentences as TRUE. All items should be marked FALSE, however, for reasons to follow.

One reason people get some answers "wrong" is that they misperceive the directions. The instructions said an item should be called FALSE if it is not *always* TRUE — an unusual definition of the word "false." From our many years of true-false tests in school we have been programmed to believe a thing is either true or false. Thus, the mere sight of the words can trigger our laying the old map upon a new territory.

The World of Progress

Another reason for error is that we can be fooled by the structure of the language. The words come across as authoritative; as factual, definite and final. But nothing in nature is totally factual, much less final. What goes on in the non-verbal world are ever-changing processes, phenomena that don't stand still. Our static language as a map doesn't fit non-verbal goings on. For example, apples are not always red; they may be green or yellow. More important, any given apple, if examined closely, will reveal several colors. Furthermore, even as we hold one under observation it changes color, becoming ever so slightly more brown. Eventually it will turn mostly brown and then black. The color of an apple depends upon its type, its age, the surface on which it is observed, and of course, upon the eyesight of the observer.

Milk is milk you say? What is *called* milk may be raw or pasteurized, containing small to lethal amounts of bacteria. If it is derived from cows, it might contain enough fat to grow a calf but bloat a baby. Mother's milk could contain immunizing agents while powdered milk could lack vitamins or contain harmful hormones. What kind of milk are we talking about? For what kind of people is it intended?

Do one and one make two? Always? Yes, but only by definition in the symbolic world of arithmetic. However, mixing one unit of alcohol with one unit of water results in something less than two units. In nature, substances when combined may mix, evaporate, synergize, turn into gas, or even explode. What, for example, would one stick of dynamite plus one lighted cigarette equal? It could be vital to know that one jigger of alcohol plus one tranquilizer might result in one driver asleep at the wheel.

Being aware that changes are not necessarily additive can keep us alert to possible disaster. For example, just one more critical remark to a spouse can trigger her act of violence. One less dessert in the prison cafeteria can be the last straw preceding a riot. One degree of warming the earth's atmosphere could flood whole geographic areas. On the positive side, one more illustration might cause a student to reorganize a thought pattern. One more effort might turn a skeptic into an ally. Adding just one more person to an organization might change the whole group's morale.

Well, you might say, the speed of sound has been known to be 741.5 miles per hour for decades. It's a scientifically accepted fact, isn't it? Yes, at least it was *considered* a fact until this year (2) when George Wong discovered the figure to be (for now) 741.1 miles per hour. A difference that matters? Not to most people. But the difference could be crucial to submarine warfare or to the engineering of aeroplanes.

We must remember that scientific formulations, equations, and facts belong to the world of maps, codes, and symbols. At a symbolic level, they may be repeated until they seem absolutely true. At the non-verbal level, however, scientists are much less sure about what is absolutely true. Habitually, they pursue the fine tuning of all standards. First, they know that measurements are rarely, if ever, identical. There are too many variations in observers, in the observing instruments, and in the things observed. Some things change just by virtue of being observed. We know that equations about the speed or size of anything represent averages and generalizations about wide variations in nature. Sound speed changes with the direction of the wind; heat and humidity can make a difference. Secondly, instruments of observation keep developing. Newton's calculations were wrong by 15%; he did not have such finely calibrated instruments as scientists have today.

Whether we use the word AIDS (or any other disease word) as one thing or as a changing process can make an enormous difference in personal hope, community attitudes and government efforts. Our best information so far (3) indicates that AIDS appears to behave differently in different persons and even in different countries. Fast moving research may change definitions of symptoms, treatment measures, and ultimately prospects for cure.

Surely, however, we can say that Ronald Reagan is a Republican. Right? Yes, but is it the truth, the whole truth, and nothing but the truth? At one time he said he was a registered Democrat. Could he now be in the process of becoming something else again? What do we mean by Republican? Does a person have to believe in every plank of the platform to *be* a Republican? If not, then how many planks of the party can he disagree with without losing his category? Are the planks of the party the same in 1986 as in 1956 or in 1886? How is Republicanism changing over time? How is Ronald Reagan changing? Might there be some political figures other than Republicans whom he'd favor and even vote for? Can we even be absolutely sure that Reagan voted for himself in the last election? The point is to be aware that any important figure may be changing in crucial ways. For example, Edmund P. Wilson, once an intelligence agent, changed into a rogue selling arms to enemies. People's political beliefs and moral values, while usually stable and predictable, can change gradually or even radically. One needs only to examine one's own history to see examples.

Subject-Predicate Language: Need for Vigilance

Let's say we have acknowledged that the six statements above are not always true. What about the six or sixteen thousand others that could be listed? No one can be expected to have enough knowledge to perceive all the possible exceptions to each one. There must be a general point to all this that can be useful to any literate person.

The secret lies in recognizing what statements like the above have in common. Notice that the structure of each sentence follows a pattern: a subject followed by a predicate. Milk is - - -. Apples are - - -. One and one make - - -. Reagan is - - -. AIDS causes - - -. What we need is to develop the habit of red-flagging such structures. We must remember the general principle that whereas nouns like apple, Reagan, and milk seem like static phenomena, what they refer to nonverbally cannot be static. Static nouns are misleading maps of territories that have, are and will be changing. Therefore, we know that what nouns are, have, or do won't stand still either. Immediately, we can adopt a skeptical stance whenever confronted by subject-predicate structures. We can then ask appropriate questions such as: When? Where? According to whom? As measured by what or whom? For whom? In what circumstances? What do they mean by? In other words, the noun-predicate structure, to be a good map of a changing territory, must be modified to reveal the dynamic variables of who, what, where, when, and in what context.

If this principle of remembering that things keep changing is important to accuracy in thinking or communicating about milk or apples, it is even more important when dealing with emotionally laden or highly abstract subjects. For example, consider such words as freedom, communism, terrorist, government official, Libya, capitalism, *The New York Times*, fundamentalist, etc. Our "languaging" them in nouns makes them seem like static things, stereotypes even. Yet each one could have multiple meanings, depending upon who uses them in what time, place, and context.

The noun "freedom," if perceived as a thing, could be falsely interpreted as something people either have or don't have. Some countries seem to have freedom while others have none at all. Adolescents can drug themselves to death in their fight for freedom from parents who they think give them no freedom. Freedom should be seen as a word reflecting many variables and many shades of meaning. Relevant questions would be: What do you and they mean by it? Freedom for whom to do what, when, how, in what circumstances? How much freedom should an 8-year-old have in a classroom, a theater, in the privacy of her own bedroom? To what extent can a government protect the freedom of business leaders to maximize profits while protecting the population's right to freedom from toxic wastes?

Take a sentence like, "Productivity improvement means lowering costs and increasing labor's output." The sentence sounds authoritative, logical, and sensible. But the subject-predicate structure ("Productivity improvement means...")

puts us on the alert. At the non-verbal level, the subject of productivity won't stand still long enough for us to take a snap-shot and offer a static picture. In fact, paradoxically, according to a *Harvard Business Review* article (4) we find that lowering costs and badgering employees to produce more is not only least effective but also vulnerable to backlash. Apparently, spending more for modern equipment, a better location and more innovative managers works better.

Antidotes for Misleading Maps

In our course, we ask the faculty to go through the motions of changing subject-predicate generalizations to fit what they realize is a changing reality. For example, you might now want to practice modifying the six sentences above. How many ways can you re-phrase "Apples are red," using the questions: According to whom? Which one? When? As measured by? In what context? etc. Now try the word "terrorist." Without practicing such modifications, tedious though they may be, we can easily remain lulled into believing the world is just like our obsolete maps.

Some people object that others don't like writing that contains qualifications. They say people prefer to know exactly what's what with no waffling. To this objection I answer that if people prefer a false sense of security, they may prefer even less to be misled by predictions that fail. Of course, when speaking of apples, multiple qualifications may be a deadly bore. The point, however, is to recognize when accuracy is important. We must not arbitrarily accept or reject the words of a politician, priest, or knave. Nouns and categories refer to events that may be neither permanent nor reliable. Knowing the specifics through asking questions improves the match between map and territory.

Summary

This article reflects one session of a course in Thinking & Communicating for Pace University faculty, a course adaptable for many other groups.

The purpose is to heighten awareness that language can seriously misrepresent the events which it describes.

Recognizing subject-predicate structures can alert us to the need for asking questions such as: According to whom? Which one? Where? At what time? In what context? etc.

NOTE AND REFERENCES

1. The Thinking & Learning Center of Pace University is endowed by Robert K. Straus in memory of J.S. Bois, A. Korzybski, J. Piaget, F.J. Roethlisberger, and Sir A. Zimmern to further students' awareness of how they perceive, evaluate and make decisions day-to-day. Subject matter is based upon a "Roots of Knowledge" approach to critical thinking. Many formulations derive from epistemics and general semantics.

2. J. Gleick, Scientist Corrects an Old Error on Hallowed Speed of Sound, *The New York Times*, June 24, 1986, page Cl.

3. M.P. Rowe, M. Russel-Einhorn, and M.A. Baker, The Fear of AIDS, *Harvard Business Review*, July-August 1986, 28.

4. W. Skinner, The Productivity Paradox, *Harvard Business Review*, July-August 1986, 55.

Alfred Korzybski founded the Institute of General Semantics in 1938. Since then, the Institute has been the world center for general semantics training. For information on upcoming seminars and other events, write to:

Institute of General Semantics
163 Engle Street
Englewood, NJ 07631

From *Et cetera* 43, no. 4 (Winter 1986) pages 349-354.

How Can We Avoid Being Mindless?

by Gregory Sawin

"S OME PEOPLE have one-track minds and have only one re- sponse to any and all problems...but [this]...is not think- ing." (1) Is such mindlessness promoted by the way we use language? Can mindful and flexible thinking be cultivated by using language in a different way? Harvard University psychologists, Ellen J. Langer and Alison I. Piper, investi- gated mindlessness versus mindfulness in a study that ad- dressed these questions. (2) In the last decade, Ellen Langer has conducted many studies on mindlessness and she pub- lished a book on this topic. (3-8)

Mindless people rigidly use information as if it has only one meaning; they are unaware of other potential meanings and tend to be less attentive to detail. In contrast, when mindful people process information, they are aware of more than one meaning and are able to make finer distinctions, attend to details, and create new categories. (9,10)

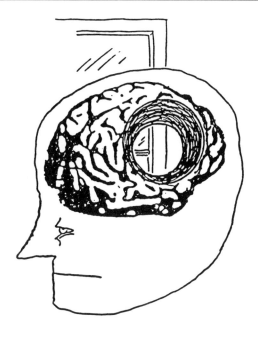

Language and Mindlessness

The results of the Langer-Piper study suggest that certain ways of using language can promote mindless evaluation of the world around us, and this can limit our ways of responding to a situation. This conclusion supports the claim of general semanticists that how we use language can have an impact on how we think. If we can learn to use language in new ways, we can cultivate mindfulness and thereby improve our ability to think in terms of degrees of probability rather than the either-or absolutes of certainty or impossibility. (11,12)

One purpose of general semantics is to promote the flexible, effective thinking that can help us avoid "hardening of the categories": He is an X and he is just like all the other Xs. (13) Sometimes use of "is" can lead people to think that if they have a label for something, they need no other information to react to it. (14,15) But with a general semantics approach, we try to consider and, if possible, observe the territory *before* creating maps or labels for it.

By using general semantics methods, we can train ourselves to make more distinctions and see more possibilities when we evaluate situations in our everyday lives. (16-19) For example, if we avoid assuming that the answer to a problem is either solution A or solution B, then we are more likely to consider other possible solutions: A and B; C alone; D alone; C and D; C followed by D, etc.

Dealing with Complexity

We live in a complex, constantly changing world filled with infinite variety. If observant, we can usually see that no two things, people, or situations are absolutely identical in all respects. (20) Regarding the endless variety and complexity of things, Korzybski claimed that our ways of thinking about them are unnecessarily limited by our use of language. (21) If we are to become more mindful, flexible thinkers, we must try to be more observant and include the details for creating more accurate mental maps.

Kung Fu Fighting?

If we mindlessly enter a situation with unexamined assumptions and expectations, such mental maps may result in counterproductive or even disastrous action.

For example, several years ago, my brother told me this true story: A kung fu student happened to notice two women in a street fight, and he tried to break it up. As he acted to separate the women, a man saw the three of them struggling. Thinking that the student was attacking the women, the man grabbed a knife and ran to their rescue — stabbing and killing the student. It seems to me that the man acted as if he had created this mental map of the situation: "The kid is attacking the women!" So, being a good citizen, his behavior logically followed — he "defended" the women.

But what if the man had started with a different mental map? "The kid *could be* attacking the women! I'll take this knife, get out there and tell him to stop." Perhaps, with this map, the man would have realized that his perception of the situation might be wrong, and it could have given him a few seconds in which to warn the kid and get more information about what was really happening. The man apparently never suspected that his mental map did not match the territory of his "reality."

REFERENCES

1. F.A. Cartier, Stop to Think — Start to Think!, *Journal of the American Dietetic Association*, Vol. 41, No. 5 (November 1962) 433.
2. E.J. Langer and A.I. Piper, The Prevention of Mindlessness, *Journal of Personality and Social Psychology*, Vol. 53 (1987) 280-287.
3. B. Chanowitz, and E. Langer, Premature Cognitive Commitment, *Journal of Personality and Social Psychology*, Vol. 41 (1981) 132-133.
4. E. Langer, P. Beck, R. Janoff-Bulman, and C. Timko, An Explanation of the Relationships Between Mindfulness, Longevity, and Senility, *Academic Psychology Bulletin*, Vol. 6 (1984) 211-226.
5. E. Langer and L. Imber, When Practice Makes Imperfect: The Debilitating Effects of Overlearning, *Journal of Personality and Social Psychology*, Vol. 37 (1979) 2014-2025.
6. E. Langer and A. Piper, Television from a Mindfulness/Mindlessness Perspective, in *Television as a Social Issue: Applied Social Psychology Annual*, Vol. 8 (Beverly Hills, CA, Sage, in press).
7. E. Langer and C. Weinman, When Thinking Disrupts Intellectual Performance: Mindlessness on an Overlearned Task, *Personality and Social Psychology Bulletin*, Vol. 7 (1981) 240-243.

8. E. Langer, *Mindfulness* (Reading, MA, Addison-Wesley, 1989).

9. E. Langer, Playing the Middle Against Both Ends: The Usefulness of Adult Cognitive Activity in Childhood and Old Age, in S. Yussen (ed.), *The Development of Reflection* (New York, Academic Press, 1983).

10. E. Langer, A. Blank and B. Chanowitz, The Mindlessness of Ostensibly Thoughtful Action, *Journal of Personality and Social Psychology*, Vol. 36 (1978) 635-642.

11. A. Korzybski, *Science and Sanity* (Englewood, NJ, Institute of General Semantics, 4th ed. 1958) 60, 107-110, 411, 506, 539-540, 559.

12. Ibid., 93, 215, 310, 405, 680, 716.

13. M. Morain (ed.), *Enriching Professional Skills Through General Semantics* (San Francisco, CA, International Society for General Semantics, 1986) xii.

14. Korzybski, 34-35, 372-373, 408-410, 478.

15. S.I. Hayakawa, *Language in Thought and Action* (New York, Harcourt Brace Jovanovich Inc., 4th ed. 1978) 199-208.

16. Korzybski, xxxv.

17. Korzybski, xxxv, xlviii-li, 13, 58,135, 386-433.

18. W. Johnson, *People in Quandaries: The Semantics of Personal Adjustment* (New York, Harper & Row, 1946; recently reprinted by the International Society for General Semantics, Concord, CA) 207-215.

19. Ibid., 116-117.

20. Korzybski, li, lxxxiv-lxxxv, 396, 427, 432, 462, 540, 565, 726.

21. Korzybski, 444-447 & 461-464.

From *Et cetera* 46, no. 3 (Fall 1989) pages 274-276.

There once lived a scribe so obtuse
He was guilty of reader abuse
It took him some time,
But he found that E-Prime
Could reduce the abstruse to good use.

—Francis A. Cartier

General Semantics as Critical Thinking: A Personal View

by Gregory Sawin

*We are witnessing the growth of a remarkable consensus that
the achievement of basic literacy...is not a sufficient goal....
[Elementary and secondary school] graduates must not only
be literate; they must also be competent thinkers.* (1)

I N 1967, at the age of 17, after a serious injury that resulted
from my own carelessness, I began to realize that much of
what happens in my life is not a matter of destiny or fate. I
am largely responsible for my patterns of evaluation and behavior. Certainly I cannot control all the events in my life,
but I believe that I can influence many of them.

The Professional Person

My injury required a long recuperation that allowed me to
think deeply about how to improve my thinking so I could
avoid unnecessary mishaps. I decided to develop a logic-
oriented way of life that was based partly on the popular *Star
Trek* character, Spock. (2) I called it my "professional person"

idea after it occurred to me that birds are better at being birds than people are at being people. Birds generally live up to their potential by building proper nests, finding food, and caring for their chicks to promote survival of the species. However, many humans, despite their tremendous potential for constructive, cooperative, and survival-oriented behavior, seemed to be falling far short of living successfully as rational beings.

Seeking Rationality

The most important thing I did to cultivate this new orientation was to become aware of my own thinking and acting. I wanted to behave more intelligently, so I began to change my patterns of thought and action that seemed irrational, impulsive, and unlikely to bring good results. I tried to learn from my mistakes and the mistakes of others. I did not want to aimlessly stumble into adulthood, which is the fate of many teenagers who become premature parents, victims of addiction, etc. I preferred to cultivate a safe, healthy, and happy lifestyle. I felt responsible for shaping myself into the kind of person I wanted to be. As much as possible, I wanted to select the direction my life would take in my journey into the future. For me, rationality was the key to achieving these goals. So, at age 17, I began to develop my own style of "critical thinking" for the sake of a better life. There are many different styles, but here is a general definition: Critical thinking is "responsible and reflective thinking that is focused upon deciding what to believe or do." (3) It also "provides standards and criteria for gaining, assessing, and using information." (4)

The Value of Critical Thinking

Why is critical thinking important? One answer is that citizens in a democracy need to be rational, educated people  who are skillful decision makers when voting or serving on a jury. Sustaining and improving our democratic way of life requires that we be active and informed citizens. S.I. Hayakawa wrote that "the task of the citizen today, to an unprecedented degree, is to distinguish sense from nonsense, confronted as we are by the greatest deluge of words that human beings have ever faced." (5) Along similar lines, Piaget maintained that "...[one] goal of education is to form minds which can be critical, can verify, and not accept everything they are offered. The great danger today is of slogans, collective opinions, ready-made trends of thoughts. We have to be able to resist individually, to criticize, to distinguish between what is proven and what is not." (6)

Critical thinking is important for yet another reason. From childhood onward, life repeatedly challenges us to cope with situations and problems that are not identical to those we dealt with in the past. If life were just a series of the same problems emerging over and over, one could mindlessly apply old solutions that worked before. But in a complex world that is constantly changing, we don't have that luxury. To increase our coping ability we need critical thinking skills to cultivate flexibility and creativity in our decision making and problem solving.

General Semantics: A System of Methods

These answers are compatible with some goals of general semantics, but I believe it is much more than just another style of critical thinking.   Charlotte Read described general semantics as "...a general theory of evaluation based on modern scientific knowledge and postulates.... The system, of which general semantics is the *modus operandi*, was called 'non-aristotelian,' as it includes and goes beyond the traditional 'aristotelian'.... It represents a method-ological synthesis of intellectual trends in the Western world that evolved during the first quarter of the twentieth century and earlier. It has both theoretical and practical aspects." (7) J.S. Bois claimed that "general semantics...attempts to organize, in a well-balanced system, the cumulative findings of the human sciences of our time and to derive from this system rules and procedures for self-management and mutual understanding." (8)

General semantics is a *system* of methods that we can use to improve our evaluating skills. As an analogy, consider that, for self-defense, a kung fu master has learned a system of blocks, punches, and kicks. If attacked, the master is likely to be more efficient and successful in dealing with the threat compared to someone without a system who knows how to throw only one punch.

The general semantics orientation should be thoroughly learned and *internalized* so that it will work automatically, like the kung fu master's system of self-defense. If attacked, his internalized system has prepared him to launch techniques to defend against various punches and kicks.

General semantics can help us to perceive, think, act, and react more intelligently and rationally in response to the stream of expected — and unexpected — events in our everyday lives.

My vision of a multiyear critical-thinking program for junior and senior high school would include general semantics, but this alone would not be sufficient. Developing listening skills would be part of the program as well.* (9) Logic and statistical thinking also would be included. Evaluating in degrees of probability, rather than in terms of certainty or impossibility, is fundamental for a critical thinker. H.G. Wells predicted that "statistical thinking will one day be as necessary for efficient citizenship as the ability to read and write." (10) Chess also could be part of such a program. "Chess playing helps children learn cause and effect, sequencing, timing, organization, patience" (11); "in chess, they must not depend on fate, but on themselves.... It stimulates intelligence, intuition, memory, imagination." (12) Such a program also should include an introduction to scientific method. (13)

Of course, there are other subjects that would be quite appropriate, but I believe that general semantics, because of its fundamental nature and its wide-ranging applicability, should be part of a critical thinking program.

NOTES AND REFERENCES

* Mary Wise, Executive Director, International Listening Association, Center for Information & Communication Sciences, Ball State University, Muncie, IN 47306.

1. L.B. Resnick and L.E. Klopfer (eds.), *Toward the Thinking Curriculum: Current Cognitive Research* (1989 Yearbook of the Association for Supervision and Curriculum Development) 1.

2. G. Sawin, In Memoriam: Gene Roddenberry, *Et cetera* 48, no. 4 (Winter 1991-1992) 452-455.

3. S.P. Norris and R.H. Ennis, *Evaluating Critical Thinking* (Pacific Grove, CA, Midwest, 1989) 1.

4. S.P. Norris, Can We Test Validly for Critical Thinking?, *Educational Researcher* 18, no. 9 (December 1989) 23.

5. S.I. Hayakawa, The Task of the Listener, in M. Morain (ed.), *Bridging Worlds through General Semantics: Selections from Et cetera (1943-1983)*, (San Francisco, International Society for General Semantics, 1984) 203.

6. R.E. Ripple and V.N. Rockcastle (eds.), *Piaget Rediscovered* (Ithaca, NY, Cornell University, 1964) 5.

7. C.S. Read, General Semantics, in M. Morain (ed.), *Bridging Worlds through General Semantics: Selections from Et cetera (1943-1983)*, 63.

8. J.S. Bois, *The Art of Awareness: A Textbook on General Semantics and Epistemics* (Dubuque, IA, Wm. C. Brown Co., 3d ed. 1978) 16-17.

9. Ibid., 290-91.

10. H.G. Wells, in S.K. Campbell, *Flaws and Fallacies in Statistical Thinking* (Englewood Cliffs, NJ, Prentice-Hall Inc., 1974) I highly recommend this 200-page introductory statistics book. In addition to being a very entertaining and readable book, it provides much valuable and highly relevant advice for people to use in avoiding faulty reasoning and for making sense of many kinds of information. From the Preface: "I have long felt that the university student...could benefit from a non-technical book written with a view to helping him increase his ability to judge the quality of statistical evidence, and in turn, to make better-informed decisions about many facets of everyday life." — Stephen K. Campbell, University of Denver.

11. *Chess Life* (March 1980) 6.

12. *Chess Life* (June 1980) 8.

13. T.M. Weiss, E.V. Moran, and E. Cottle, *Education for Adaptation and Survival* (San Francisco, International Society for General Semantics, 1975) xv.

From *Et cetera* 48, no. 3 (Fall 1991) pages 306-309.

Q: What aspect of the general semantics approach is particularly appealing to you?

A: Its recognition of the importance of change — the acknowledgment that our ideas, our understanding, need not be frozen in time, but, with the gaining of new experience and knowledge, are open to review. And, of course, general semantics theory and practice are themselves subject to revision. In these respects, general semantics offers a link between some of the more advanced lines of modern thought and life as we live it.

—Jeremy Klein
Editor-in-Chief
Et cetera
(From an interview)

Chess, Science, and General Semantics

by Gregory Sawin

W HAT DO CHESS PLAYING, the practice of scientific method, and the application of general semantics principles have in common? Each activity requires systematic, clear thinking in pursuit of reliable knowledge.

Scientific Method

First, consider science. The products of science abound: computers, laser beams, world-wide communication networks, sophisticated surgical procedures, robots, spacecraft, etc. Perhaps, for many people, these come to mind when they think about science. But, for me, the essence of science is not high technology — it is *method*. The ways of thinking and the various procedures known as "the scientific method," developed and refined over many generations, are what made these technologies possible.

Scientific methods include, but are not limited to, careful observation, recording what was observed, generating possible explanations, designing and conducting experiments to

Adapted portion of "Metamorphose" (1940) by M. C. Escher.
G. W. Breughel/Reprinter, 1427 AP Amstelhoek, Holland.

gain more information about the process under study, followed by new or revised explanations of the process that more adequately account for the observed results. In addition, such procedures require careful use of symbol systems, such as language (including scientific terminology) and mathematics, to enable researchers to communicate accurately to other scientists the procedures, measurements, and results of experiments. I view scientific method as an approach to acquiring reliable knowledge about energies, forces, substances, and life-forms.

Much of general semantics is based on scientific procedures and findings: 1) We, and the universe around us, consist of dynamic molecular, atomic, and subatomic processes that constantly change. 2) To learn about processes, we should study them, search for "facts," and try to discover relationships between facts. 3) Words are not as important as facts. Ultimately, authority resides in facts, not words. If someone claims that a statement corresponds to a fact, then it must be supported by evidence if it is to be considered as reliable knowledge. 4) Descriptions should be tailored to fit the facts. We should not distort or ignore the facts for the sake of perpetuating preconceived notions or wishful thinking. As rational beings, one of our responsibilities is to reckon with the facts. 5) An inference is an assertion or guess that goes beyond what is known about something based on a description of the facts. We should learn to recognize the difference between a descriptive statement and an inferential statement.

Practitioners of science or general semantics strive for rigor in the use of symbol systems — their verbal reports of observations, measurements, inferences, and theories should correspond to what was discovered regarding the non-verbal processes being studied. Scientists and general semanticists can make observations, develop ideas, and draw conclusions, but, typically, they are willing to revise their statements when new evidence requires it.

General Semantics

I regard general semantics as a science-oriented approach to improving human functioning on several levels. Human life is so much more than simply a matter of dealing with physical realities of the moment. Not only do we live in the present, we also learn about the past and anticipate the future. From birth we have been shaped by challenges and opportunities offered by our physical environments. In addition, through various modes of communication, we were also molded by our social environments — the people of the past and present who conveyed to us various reports of their experiences, knowledge, beliefs, etc. How we make sense of the world and cope with reality is influenced by patterns of thinking and living passed down to us by older generations.

General semantics was developed to help us function more successfully as humans — that profoundly interdependent community of communicators — so we could build a brighter future for ourselves and humanity in general. To function more effectively, our goal should be to learn about 1) the apparently universal characteristics of reality (such as the process of constant change in all things and no two things being literally "identical"), 2) how we function — in terms of perception, physiology, neurology, psychology, and social behavior, 3) better ways of using language so our thinking will be more coordinated with reality and our behavior will be more appropriate to the situation, and 4) how we can communicate more skillfully with others to promote cooperation and mutual understanding.

Chess

I think chess playing, in principle, is similar to practicing scientific method or general semantics. The object in chess is to win the game by rationally dealing with problems that your opponent creates for you, and by formulating and launching attacks that will eventually checkmate your opponent.

The basic method of playing chess requires close observation of the facts — the relations between your pieces and your opponent's pieces, the relations among your own pieces and among your opponent's pieces on the board, how these positions are interrelated, and how the interrelations change from move to move. After understanding such relationships and their implications, you have a basis for making moves to improve your pawn structure, bait your opponent into making a mistake, bolster your defense, develop an attack, etc. As you make a move, you can use chess notation to record it on paper so you can later replay and analyze the game. You watch your opponent's move, record it, and try to discover the possible consequences of the move — for you *and* the opponent — in terms of opportunities or threats in this new position, then you choose the best move among those you are considering, you make that move, and so on.

This is similar to some aspects of scientific method: In seeking reliable information during a chess game, a player: 1) carefully observes the position, 2) tries to generate several possible explanations for the purpose of the opponent's move, 3) develops short-term and long-term strategies based on the apparent positional strengths and weaknesses of both contestants, and 4) evaluates the soundness of those ideas by imagining possible positions several moves ahead. By learning the methods of chess, one can become acquainted with the concepts of probability, alternative courses of action, cause and effect, and the links between clear thinking, effective behavior and good results.

Skillful chess playing does not happen as a result of impulsive moves made without regard to the position on the board and the principles of good chess. General semantics, scientific method, and chess playing require the self-discipline to consistently apply a method — a system of techniques to be used according to principles that apply in various kinds of situations.

To summarize, using the methods of chess, science, or general semantics can cultivate rational thinking for the sake of gaining reliable knowledge. Such methods can serve as tools for building more successful futures — in games or in life.

From *Et cetera* 49, no. 1 (Spring 1992) pages 104-107.

"I, myself, find it hard to resist the temptation to define the educated woman in terms of what she knows. Instead, we are trying to evolve standards by which we can evaluate the education of a woman in answering other questions — not only what does she know, but how does she apply her knowledge? .... What are her standards of values by which she measures life and people, and makes her selections? We hope that the outcomes of the Barstow education can be evaluated in answering these questions in terms of the best potentialities of human nature."

—Marjorie Mercer Kendig

Headmistress, Barstow School for Girls, Kansas City, Missouri (1934–1938). Educational Director, Institute of General Semantics (1938–1950). Director, Institute of General Semantics (1950–1965 & 1971–1975).

(Excerpt from address delivered on March 17, 1937, reprinted in the *General Semantics Bulletin* (1983) No. 50, p. 43; tracing based on photo in same issue of the *General Semantics Bulletin*; Institute of General Semantics, Englewood, New Jersey.)

It Never Occurred to Me

by Gregory Sawin

BANG-BANG! You're dead! Two young brothers went to an amusement park. They eventually wandered to the shooting gallery and one boy took a few shots at the moving targets; then he playfully pointed the rifle at his brother, fired it, and killed him. It was supposed to be just a thoughtless, harmless act — if the boy with the gun had suspected that it could hurt his brother, he wouldn't have done it. But apparently, he assumed that the gun was some sort of toy that couldn't hurt anyone. He probably wasn't even aware that he was making an assumption and that this assumption could be wrong. I suspect that his logic was not faulty, but his thinking and action followed from an incorrect *hidden assumption*.

I believe that most behavior is dictated by logic that sprouts from assumptions — including hidden assumptions. Logic alone is not sufficient to enable one to come to a sensible conclusion. If the assumptions are false, the logic based on those assumptions just cranks out false conclusions — it is easy to

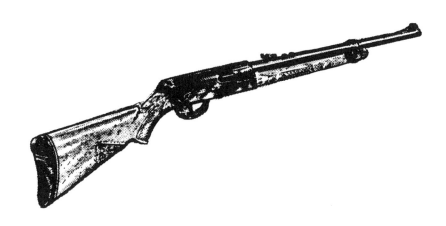

be logical but wrong. General semantics is a system for rational living that goes beyond logic. Korzybski put it this way: "General semantics is not any 'philosophy,' or 'psychology,' or 'logic,' in the ordinary sense. It is a new...discipline which...trains us...to use our nervous systems most efficiently." (1) Many general semanticists are concerned about how hidden assumptions may interfere with skillful thinking and successful living.

Perhaps the first person to suspect the existence of hidden assumptions was Saint Augustine (A.D. 354-430), who "recognized the presuppositions one takes for granted in any thinking, even the asking of a question." (2) Along similar lines, Korzybski wrote: "Our habits of speech become part of our data, and represent already preconceived ideas." (3) He claimed that "underlying... assumptions and implications... are silently hidden behind our languages.... These assumptions... may be called 'unconscious,' because they are totally unknown and unsuspected.... Any form of representation has its own...assumptions... and when we accept a language we unconsciously accept sets of... assumptions of which we become semantic victims." (4)   Korzybski was not alone in thinking this way. The philosopher John Dewey wrote, "We discover that we believe many things not because the things are so, but because we have become habituated through... the unconscious effect of language, etc." (5)   Korzybski wanted us to become aware of some hidden assumptions that can cause us to make mental errors and act or react incorrectly.

He based general semantics on his idea that humanity is a special form of life — we are "time-binders." (6)   Our ability to create, use, and teach complex languages gives us great power to bind time: We accumulate knowledge from the past, exchange it, expand it, and apply it in the present, and we transmit it to the next generation.   Hayakawa contended that "man, as a symbol-creating and symbol-using class of life, reflects the structure of his symbol-systems [languages] in the structure of his reaction-patterns." (7)   Language has given us the freedom to become powerful time-binders but, due to the influence of hidden assumptions, our language still makes us prisoners by limiting the flexibility of our thinking.

Perception-based Hidden Assumptions

Dewey wrote: "In spite of the acute and penetrating powers of observation among the Greeks, their 'science' is a

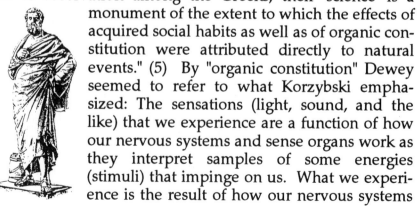

monument of the extent to which the effects of acquired social habits as well as of organic constitution were attributed directly to natural events." (5)   By "organic constitution" Dewey seemed to refer to what Korzybski emphasized: The sensations (light, sound, and the like) that we experience are a function of how our nervous systems and sense organs work as they interpret samples of some energies (stimuli) that impinge on us.   What we experience is the result of how our nervous systems make sense of those energies. (8-10) The ancient Greeks, and many people in today's world, acquired the hidden assumption that how they see the world is how it *is*. But, of course, no one can get outside the limitations of one's nervous system to see reality with absolute objectivity. If we could do this, we would never be fooled by magicians or optical illusions (11,12), and we would never misinterpret a situation. (13,14) Hayakawa explained that "Experience does not tell us what it is that we are experiencing." (15)

Culture-based Hidden Assumptions

The Chinese philosopher Chang Tung-Sun declared that "All thought, in addition to being influenced by our immediate social environment, is also molded by our remote cultural heritage. The immediate forces determine the trend of our thought, while the remote cultural heritage determines the forms in which thought is made possible." (16) Hayakawa maintained that "We all develop, knowingly or unknowingly, conceptual frameworks which help us understand the world.... It is through concepts that we are able to make sense of experience." (17) The anthropologist  Alan Dundes wrote: "There is agreement...that culture is acquired and learned.... Another characteristic of culture is that it may be unconscious... [meaning] that man is not conscious of all aspects of his culture.... It is all around us; it shapes our lives and thought; yet we know relatively little about it. One reason for studying culture is to make the unconscious conscious. By making the unconscious content of culture conscious, we may, at least in theory, be better able to do something about controlling or changing it." (18) Korzybski warned that the "...first words with which mankind started its vocabulary were labels for prescientific ideas, naive generalizations full of silent assumptions.... Our daily speech...is one enormous system of such assumptions. The moment assumptions are introduced, and it is impossible to avoid them, logical destiny begins its work; and if we do not go back all the time, uncover and discover our conscious or unconscious fundamental assumptions and revise them, mental impasses permanently obstruct the way." (19) One reason he developed general semantics was to "help mankind *select* their lot *consciously*." (20)

Language-based Hidden Assumptions

Although it may be illegitimate to treat culture and language as separate processes because they are so thoroughly interrelated, for the purpose of analysis I have separated them.

Language behavior is so deeply interwoven in the fabric of our lives that we grow up failing to make a sharp distinction between our world of words and our world of not-words — our perceptions of the things and happenings around us. (21,22) I think most of us innocently acquired the false hidden assumption of a special kind of "connection" between symbols (words, numbers, etc.) and reality. This assumed connection is obvious in superstitions, such as the belief that "13" is unlucky; so some buildings have no floor numbered 13. (23)

Less obvious is that in their day-to-day dealings with life, many people seem to behave on the basis of this assumed connection between words and reality. For example, some believe that a verbal insult requires a violent response. But words alone can't change people: "Can I make you what I call you just by calling you that? Of course not." (24)

Another false hidden assumption is that all words are meaningful. Many people apparently assume that if a word exists, then there must be a thing in reality that corresponds to the word. Korzybski distinguished between "words" that represent real things (or processes) and "noises," counterfeit symbols that correspond to nothing real. Related to this "words vs. noises" problem is the fact that some people automatically assume that there is an answer to every question. If you agree with that idea, then provide a sensible or meaningful answer to this question: "How many fairies can dance on the head of a unicorn?" (25) Nonsense questions that contain meaningless noises cannot have meaningful answers. When dealing with information, if we fail to distinguish between words and noises, we can be misled and come to the wrong conclusions.

One more false hidden assumption is that words tell us *all* about something, so a statement about some thing is just as important as the thing itself — map equals territory. Therefore, you don't need to look at the territory, just look at someone's word-map of it. This wrong-headed idea relates to labeling people. Some people seem to think that once you know how someone is labeled, you know what the person *is*, so just look at the label, not the person, for information on how to judge him or her. (26)

Hidden Assumptions and Choice

The danger of hidden assumptions is that without training, we usually don't suspect them. (27-33) We don't know about them; we don't think about them; we don't talk about them — but they do influence us. I imagine that many persuaders and manipulators know how to cultivate certain hidden assumptions to sell their products or points of view. Thus, if only in self-defense, it should benefit us to become aware of the possibility of hidden assumptions so that we can make rational, conscious choices in life.

Conclusion

We can examine our conscious assumptions before we employ logic based on them, but these conscious assumptions are based on our hidden assumptions that we can't examine until we discover them. How do we do that? One way is to use the general semantics approach to rational living to cultivate greater awareness of factors that can influence our perceiving, evaluating, and behaving.

REFERENCES

1. A. Korzybski, *Science and Sanity* (Englewood, NJ, Institute of General Semantics, 4th ed. 1958) xxvi.

2. S.I. Berman, Aristotelian, Non-aristotelian Logic and Korzybski's Psychologics, in S.I. Berman (ed.), *Logic and General Semantics: Writings of Oliver L. Reiser and Others* (San Francisco, International Society for General Semantics, 1989) 152.

3. A. Korzybski, *Time-Binding: The General Theory* [two papers: 1924 and 1926], (Englewood, NJ, Institute of General Semantics, 10th printing 1981) [1926] 42.

4. Korzybski, *Science and Sanity*, 506.

5. J. Dewey, *Experience and Nature* (New York, Dover, 1958) 14. (This book contains the Paul Carus series of lectures delivered by Dewey in 1925.)

6. A. Korzybski, *Manhood of Humanity* (Englewood, NJ, Institute of General Semantics, 2d ed. 1950).

7. S.I. Hayakawa, Reply to Professor Bures, in S.I. Berman (ed.), *Logic and General Semantics: Writings of Oliver L. Reiser and Others*, 148.

8. Korzybski, *Science and Sanity*, 235-39, 376, 382-83.

9. R. Rivlin and K. Gravelle, *Deciphering the Senses: The Expanding World of Human Perception* (New York, Simon and Schuster, 1984).

10. R.L. Gregory, *Eye and Brain: The Psychology of Seeing* (New York, World University Library/McGraw-Hill, 1966) 44-46, 62, 68-71.

11. Rivlin and Gravelle, *Deciphering the Senses*, 159-71.

12. Gregory, *Eye and Brain*, 131-63, 178-82.

13. Korzybski, *Science and Sanity*, xxxiv-xxxv.

14. A. Linkletter, *Oops! Or, Life's Awful Moments* (New York, Pocket Books, 1969).

15. S.I. Hayakawa, *Language in Thought and Action* (New York, Harcourt Brace Jovanovich, 4th ed. 1978) 291.

16. T.S. Chang, A Chinese Philosopher's Theory of Knowledge, in S.I. Berman (ed.), *Logic and General Semantics: Writings of Oliver L. Reiser and Others,* 116.

17. Hayakawa, *Language in Thought and Action,* 292.

18. A. Dundes, *Every Man His Way: Readings in Cultural Anthropology* (Englewood Cliffs, NJ, Prentice-Hall, 1968) 158.

19. A. Korzybski, Fate and Freedom, in I.J. Lee (ed.), *The Language of Wisdom and Folly* (New York, Harper, 1949) 346.

20. Korzybski, *Science and Sanity,* 273.

21. W. Johnson, *People in Quandaries: The Semantics of Personal Adjustment* (New York, Harper & Brothers, 1946; recently reprinted by the International Society for General Semantics, Concord, CA) 91-142.

22. Hayakawa, *Language in Thought and Action,* 12-16, 172-78.

23. Ibid., 27.

24. A. Fleishman, Dialogue with a Street Fighter, in M. Morain (ed.), *Enriching Professional Skills through General Semantics: Selections from Et cetera* (San Francisco, International Society for General Semantics, 1986) 40.

25. Korzybski, *Science and Sanity,* 63, 78-83, 138.

26. Hayakawa, *Language in Thought and Action,* 200-209.

27. F.P. Chisholm, *Introductory Lectures on General Semantics* (Englewood, NJ, Institute of General Semantics, 13th printing 1980) 8, 10-14, 19, 27-30.

28. M. Morain (ed.), *Teaching General Semantics: A Collection of Lesson Plans for College and Adult Classes* (San Francisco, International Society for General Semantics, 1969) 1-21, 105-18, 128.

29. Korzybski, *Science and Sanity*, 60, 93, 110, 130, 279, 419, 448, 483-84, 505-7, 540, 544, 655.

30. Korzybski, *Time-Binding*, [1924] 21; [1926] 10, 16-17, 21-22, 26, 28, 37-38, 46.

31. J.S. Bois, *The Art of Awareness: A Textbook on General Semantics and Epistemics* (Dubuque, IA, William C. Brown, 3d ed. 1978) 141-42, 182, 189, 283.

32. A. Korzybski, *General Semantics Seminar 1937: Transcription of Notes from Lectures in General Semantics Given at Olivet College* (Englewood, NJ, Institute of General Semantics) 17, 86.

33. H.L. Weinberg, *Levels of Knowing and Existence: Studies in General Semantics* (Englewood, NJ, Institute of General Semantics, 2d ed. 1973) 15-23.

From *Et cetera* 47, no. 2 (Summer 1990) pages 181-185.

"We shall require a substantially new manner of thinking if mankind is to survive."

—Albert Einstein

Critical Thinking for Survival in the 21st Century *

by Kenneth G. Johnson

*Often what passes for logic or "critical thinking"
consists of blindly following the assumptions and
logical patterns built into our language.*

O UR SCHOOLS generally teach grammar, spelling and punctuation, but very little about the nature of language, the potentials and limitations of that remarkable human invention, not only for communicating with others, but for the communicating we do with ourselves — usually called thinking.

Logic

The average four-year-old child can do an Aristotelian syllogism with his eyes closed. He knows Toby is a cat and cats are animals. So he concludes, logically enough, that Toby is an animal. He learned that as he learned his language.

*Copyright 1986, Institute of General Semantics. Prepared for a conference of the World Future Society, New York, NY, July 14-17, 1986.

Most college graduates take that same "everyday" logic for granted. They give little thought to their assumptions about language or the assumptions embedded in the language they use. Often what passes for logic or critical thinking consists of blindly following the assumptions and logical patterns built into the language.

Hidden Assumptions

Alfred Korzybski, Polish scientist and founder of the field of general semantics, recognized that "...a language, any language, has at its bottom certain metaphysics, which ascribe, consciously or unconsciously, some sort of structure to this world.... Now these structural assumptions and implications are inside our skins when we accept a language — any language. If unraveled, they become conscious; if not, they remain unconscious." (1)

The very fact that many of these assumptions remain unconscious gives them their power. One can hardly claim to be doing "critical thinking" when much of the process is buried in hidden assumptions. General semantics focuses on the assumptions underlying symbol systems, with the relation of language to "reality," of word to fact, of theory to description, and of description to observation. It takes into account the perceptions, expectations, and previous experiences of the observer. It investigates how we know what we claim to know. It deals with the role of language in critical thinking-evaluating and in achieving predictability.

By studying the language behavior of scientists and of mental patients, Korzybski was able to abstract significant features of scientific behavior that increased predictability. He found that science and sanity, indeed our very survival, depend on predictability — on having symbolic maps similar in structure to the territory they purport to represent.

To survive in the 21st century we will need new technologies to deal with an array of new challenges: food supplies for a burgeoning population; disease; pollution; nuclear waste; urban congestion; etc. But we will also need new thinking skills, unshackled from the primitive assumptions woven into the structure of our language. "Knowing about" those assumptions will not suffice; we must retrain our nervous systems, "reprogram our bio-computers," so to speak. "Critical thinking" must not be limited to laboratories and think tanks; it is crucial in dealing with family problems, poverty, politics, ethics, interpersonal and international relations and a multitude of other problems, some yet to emerge.

The Structure of Our Language

What are some of the assumptions about language or embedded in the structure of our language that may deter effective dealings with emergent problems?

We talk about "the way things *are*," "telling it like it *is*" — forgetting, because of the undertow of habitual language structure, how Einstein and Heisenberg demonstrated that we can only talk about *our* reactions, *our* categories for what *we* abstract. The observer, using his unique nervous system, describes the event, reacts to the event, disturbs the event. But in our "to be"-oriented language, the observer disappears. Statements appear factual, absolute, static. Qualities seem to exist in things, quite apart from the observer: "He *is* schizophrenic." "They *are* a threat to us." "We *are* right; they *are* wrong." "I *am* a failure." We may, of course, have good reasons for our views, but they remain *our views*. We do not reduce conflict, tensions, misunderstandings or disagreements by talking in absolutes.

Scientists have had to invent new languages (including mathematics), not merely new words, to deal with complex inter-relationships that are poorly represented by the subject-predicate structure of our language. For example, "I will teach you" implies I will be doing the acting; you will be acted upon. "We will destroy them" contains no hint that something will happen to us in the process. We need to develop a more transactional language or, at least, become much more aware of the limitations of the subject-predicate form.

The very fact that we can put things into categories emphasizes their similarity (doctors, Russians, bureaucrats, women, blacks). Letting our language habits substitute for thinking, we may talk as if, act as if, "they're all alike." The pervasiveness of prejudice indicates to me the insidiousness of undifferentiated categories. The scholastics, following Aristotle, made the "law of identity" A is A — the first "law of thought." Korzybski proposed the premise of non-identity — A_1 is not A_2. The simple device of indexing, borrowed from mathematics, reminds us of the differences within the categories. The device can actually be used in writing or speaking, but, most important, it can be used internally to promote critical (and creative) thinking.

I sometimes give my students a list of words and ask them to give an opposite, then a word in between. The list might include *wise, selfish, sick, ambitious, lazy, alive*. They quickly discover that our language makes it easy to talk about extremes; it takes much more effort to talk (and think) about the in-betweens.   This two-valued language encourages either-or, black-or-white thinking.   General semantics encourages students to adopt a more scientific orientation, to talk and think in terms of degrees and probability.

Texts on critical thinking often suggest we begin by stating the problem and describing the situation. Then we are likely to focus our attention on these verbal maps. We may forget that these maps are not the territory. The limitations of our senses, of our nervous systems, and of our language make it clear that we cannot say *all* about anything. To complicate things further, our verbal maps provide rather static pictures of a dynamic, process world in which technology, growing at an exponential rate, changes all aspects of our society. While no magic cure, it helps to (a) be aware of the limitations of our maps, (b) recognize that every map includes the abstractions and values of the map maker, and (c) check maps against the territories they are intended to represent.

Consciousness of Abstracting

Language enables us to talk at many different orders of abstraction — descriptions, inferences, judgments, generalizations, interpretations, predictions, etc.   Few students are educated to make sharp distinctions between orders. Some react to words as if they were things and become upset by *talk* about spiders or snakes. Many react to the high-order abstractions of politicians as if they were "facts" and defend their view of the world as if it were the only correct view. To counteract such tendencies, general semantics stresses "consciousness of abstracting" and promotes an awareness of different orders of abstraction.

Self-Reflexiveness

As humans, we not only are aware, we are aware of our awareness. We react not only to our environment, but to our reactions — and our reactions to our reactions. We can think — and think about how we think, evaluate our evaluations, fear our fears, or be depressed by our feelings of depression. Language is similarly self-reflexive: we can make statements about statements; we can use language to talk about language.

The self-reflexiveness of language and the human nervous system provides us with an open-ended system that makes both creative and critical thinking, and also destructive thinking, possible. We can write poetry, spin out complex tales of fiction, plan buildings or enterprises, solve problems, conduct scientific research — or spread rumors, spin webs of delusion, and talk ourselves into insanity or war.

Self-reflexive statements that specifically refer to the language of the previous statement are called "meta-linguistic." For example, a patient might say, "I am a failure." A therapist, in his best non-directive manner, may reply, "You feel you are a failure." That is a meta-linguistic statement. It has taken a "statement of fact" (from the patient's point of view) and labeled it a *feeling*.

General semantics provides a meta-linguistic or "second-order" approach to both critical and creative thinking. It enables us to use self-reflexiveness *systematically* to monitor our ongoing evaluations. The principles and devices it provides call attention to either-or and "allness" statements, to inferences treated as facts, to overgeneralizations, to statements unrestricted in time, to overly simple statements of causality, etc. Whatever the order of abstraction, whatever the source of the statement, it can be analyzed.

Educators have developed many valuable approaches to critical thinking. General semantics does not replace these approaches, but adds an emphasis on the *critical* roles of the process of abstracting and the structure of language.

REFERENCE

1. A. Korzybski, *Science and Sanity* (Englewood, NJ, Institute of General Semantics, 4th ed. 1958) 89.

From *Et cetera* 43, no. 4 (Winter 1986) pages 358-362.

Relevant?

by Kenneth G. Johnson

MY COLLEAGUE glanced at the new book on my desk — *Alfred Korzybski: Collected Writings, 1920-1950.* (1)

"Korzybski? Is that stuff still relevant?" he asked.

I knew he was pulling my leg. He knew I had taught general semantics for more than thirty years. He knew I would not call Korzybski's work irrelevant.

An answer, both flip and brief, silenced him. But his question got me thinking. Why does Korzybski's work continue to be relevant almost sixty years after the publication of *Science and Sanity*? (2)

Science and Sanity, you may remember, came out in 1933 as a formidable tome published privately by a largely unknown author — an independent scholar who lacked the "proper" academic credentials. It didn't fit the categories revered in academia — not quite philosophy, or linguistics, or psychology, or logic, or neurology, or mathematics — yet borrowing from all of these and more. Many dismissed it without bothering to read it. Some who read it saw nothing new.

ALFRED
KORZYBSKI

COLLECTED WRITINGS
1920-1950

Collected and Arranged by

M. KENDIG

International
Non-Aristotelian
Library

INSTITUTE OF GENERAL SEMANTIC **Alfred Korzybski**

Fourth Edition
With Preface by Russell Meyers, M. D.

SCIENCE
AND
SANITY

INTRODUCTION TO NON-ARISTOTELIAN
SYSTEMS AND GENERAL SEMANTICS

BY

ALFRED KORZYBSKI
AUTHOR, *Manhood of Humanity*
FOUNDER, INSTITUTE OF GENERAL SEMANTICS

(Drawing based on a photo by Lotte Jacobi)

Somehow it inspired many popularizations, over a hundred and fifty doctoral dissertations, and two scholarly journals, as well as many college and university courses, international conferences, and seminars. His work seems as relevant today as it did in 1933 — and, in some respects, more in tune with the times. Why?

My answer, of course, involves my interests, my experiences, my interpretations. (The map necessarily includes the mapmaker.) Others would undoubtedly emphasize different reasons.

General Semantics as a System

Korzybski did not attempt to give us answers to the questions that plague us. He provided an open-ended meta-linguistic *system* for finding answers, for taking into account the nature of language and the critical role of the human nervous system.

By a system I mean a collection of related elements. Many, perhaps most, of the elements Korzybski integrated were not new. Many, apart from the system he created, seem simple, trivial, commonsensical. Only as we see the interrelatedness of the elements do we begin to sense the power and the originality of the system.

Korzybski made the human being the central element of his system. He saw mathematics or science or art — all of the fragments of a curriculum — as functions of unique human nervous systems. He insisted on putting the human into every equation.

He recognized the vital role of language in the time-binding process — the process that distinguishes human from animal. He saw self-reflexive language as a product of the self-reflexive human nervous system.

Humans not only know about their environments, they know that they know; they can think about how they think, evaluate their evaluations. Languages, too, have this self-reflexive characteristic. They enable us to talk about talk, make statements about statements, write books on writing books.

Korzybski claimed that some second-order reactions (thinking about thinking, reasoning about reasoning, evaluating our evaluations, etc.) represent healthy uses of self-reflexiveness. Others (worry about worry, fear of fear, belief in belief, etc.) represent morbid semantic reactions. He then developed a *system* for using self-reflexiveness in healthier ways, by means of such tools as the structural differential, extensional devices, consciousness of abstracting, varying the levels of abstraction, and the related formulations.

Other tools call attention to either-or and "allness" statements, to inferences treated as facts, to overgeneralizations, to multiordinal terms, to statements unrestricted in time, to overly-simple statements of causality, etc. They enable us to monitor our ongoing input and output — whether speaking, writing, listening, reading, or the critical talking-to-ourselves we usually call "thinking." The tools can be used, whatever the order of abstraction, whatever the source of the statement.

Korzybski showed much less interest in the "abstractness" of language than in the *process* of abstracting by the human nervous system. His system, like the theory of relativity, focused attention on the observer, the human factor so often lost in preoccupation with subject matter, with "objectivity."

Consciousness of Abstracting

Consciousness of that process of abstracting, when internalized, can cause dramatic changes in perspective. We become aware that the "realities" we have taken for granted were to a significant degree our own creations. We empower ourselves to re-create them. Changes that seemed impossible sometimes become simple.

Too often we accept certain premises, certain assumptions, as "given" and work within that system. General semantics, by providing tools for effective use of self-reflexiveness, enables us to challenge and go beyond the limits imposed by those assumptions.

In this brief statement I have emphasized some of the characteristics of Korzybski's system that I believe make it unique and relevant today. In a process world we must expect change, but the basic structure of the system, I believe, will be relevant for years to come.

REFERENCES

1. M. Kendig (ed.), *Alfred Korzybski: Collected Writings, 1920-1950* (Englewood NJ, Institute of General Semantics, 1990).
2. A. Korzybski, *Science and Sanity* (Englewood, NJ, Institute of General Semantics, 4th ed. 1958).

From *Et cetera* 48, no. 1 (Spring 1991) pages 59-61.

General Semantics and Intercultural Communication *

by Mitsuko Saito-Fukunaga

S EVERAL YEARS AGO, while conducting some research in my neighboring country, Korea, I heard from an influential Korean journalist about a little incident in Seoul.

At the grand opening of the Lotte Department Store, which is a joint venture of Japan and Korea, Korean sales clerks bowed deeply, Japanese-style, to greet Korean dignitaries. In Japan, department stores train their employees very carefully to treat customers in the most polite fashion; the Japanese managers had trained the Korean employees accordingly. The dignitaries and invitees at the opening felt very strange to see Korean sales clerks bowing deeply in Japanese style. The sight struck them as artificial and distasteful since it was not the Korean way. On the following day in the newspapers, there was a big write-up headed, "CULTURAL INVASION."

---

* Excerpted from a speech delivered at the United Nations meeting of Non-Governmental Organizations in 1985.

160

Upon hearing this information, I was surprised to learn that the Koreans do *not* bow deeply as a formal greeting at an initial meeting with dignitaries. Since Seoul is only two hours away from Tokyo by air, the Japanese never dreamed that their way of bowing deeply would appear strange to the Korean people.

The Headline Is Not the Territory

When I saw the newspaper headline, "CULTURAL INVASION," I felt hurt. To me it was simple ignorance on the part of the Japanese managers, far from a "cultural invasion," I am confident that Japanese business people try to maintain a sincere attitude toward joint ventures in Korea.

Why was I hurt by the newspaper headline? At the moment I forgot to apply one of the basic principles of general semantics: "The map is not the territory." The words "cultural invasion" are just words (a map), not to be confused with the intentions of the Japanese people (the territory to which the words refer). These words did not represent the Japanese managers' intentions. Because I carelessly and quickly identified the map with the territory, my feelings were hurt.

It is our task to differentiate words from nonverbal facts, the map from the territory. If we have awareness, we can observe more accurately, report more objectively and less emotionally. Our knowledge of general semantics principles can help us engage in healthier, saner communication. Had the Korean journalists some knowledge of general semantics, they might have avoided their early conclusion and chosen words other than "cultural invasion."

Fortunately, the Korean telling me of the incident seemed to believe that the Japanese were sincere but just didn't know the Korean culture. At the same time, he indicated that the newspaper headline was a consequence of ignorance of another culture.

Cultural Ignorance

How do we react when other people display ignorance of our culture? Usually by feeling unpleasant, disgusted or sometimes a bit hurt. I have found that a knowledge of general semantics principles can play an essential role in understanding and improving intercultural communication.

The first basic principle of general semantics — the map is not the territory — means that the verbal world cannot be equated with the nonverbal world, with its complex structures so diverse, heterogeneous and multifarious. Remaining aware of this principle helps insure successful communication at the intercultural level.

Another principle needing emphasis is that the map does not cover all of the territory. The map, "cultural invasion," could not show us all of what the Korean journalists meant. Looking back to the historical relationship between the two countries, there is much to consider. Remembering that the conclusions we reach, the decisions we make, are based on only part of the relevant evidence will help us keep open-minded, better prepared to discover and accept additional information.

Intercultural Communication

In our age of intercultural communication, the role of listener is very important — just as in baseball the catcher is as important as the pitcher. Listening to people with different cultural backgrounds is not only hearing and evaluating what they say. Intercultural listening means making an effort to understand what we do not understand.

In *Handling Barriers in Communication*, Irving J. Lee tells us how to avoid other possible errors. (1) Instead of searching for what "words mean," look for what "people mean." Instead of "words are containers of meaning," assume that "people are containers of meaning." He emphasizes that it is a mistake to assume that the speaker is using words the same way the listener would if the listener were doing the talking. Words, according to Lee, are just pointers used by individuals because people perceive differently.

Seeing Differently, Evaluating Differently

Here are some examples that have been used to illustrate individual differences in perception. In the first figure, some people see a duck, some people see a rabbit, and others alternately see a duck and a rabbit. In the second picture, some see the profile of an Indian while others see the back of an Eskimo walking away, and still others alternately see both. (2)

From responding to these pictures, we can gather that people *see differently* and *evaluate differently*. Such an understanding helps form the basis for successful intercultural communication.

I have learned that what may strike us as the peculiarities of a culture are often the most beloved and precious properties of the people immersed in that culture. They become peculiarities, strange experiences or shocking phenomena to outsiders only when outsiders are not prepared to accept and tolerate them.

Handy General Semantics Tools

In dealing with members of another culture, extensional** devices can be used to help enable the listener to distinguish and react to nonverbal realities instead of verbal expressions. The five such devices briefly mentioned below are useful aids in keeping our minds open when listening and speaking.

Use "et cetera" as a reminder that people cannot say or know all about anything; use indexing to show that no two things are identical; use dating to show that no one thing is ever twice the same; use quotation marks as a reminder that a word is not being used in its usual sense; and use hyphens to unite elemental*** terms to produce non-elemental terms. This summary of extensional devices draws from *General Semantics: An Outline Survey* by Kenneth Johnson. (3)

Using these devices will help improve mutual understanding in intercultural communication.

NOTES AND REFERENCES

** Editor's note: "Extensional" means fact-oriented (rather than word-oriented).

*** Editor's note: "Elemental" (or elementalistic) means using words in a way that falsely separates processes that in reality cannot be divided. For example, to say "space and time" or "heredity and environment" is elementalistic. One does not exist without the other. Such statements create false maps of reality. (4)

1. I.J. Lee and L.L. Lee, *Handling Barriers in Communication* (New York, Harper, 1957).

2. J.R. Block, H.E. Yuker, *Can You Believe Your Eyes?* (New York, Gardner Press, Inc., 1989) Also available from the International Society for General Semantics.

3. K.G. Johnson, *General Semantics: An Outline Survey* (San Francisco, International Society for General Semantics, 1972).

4. A. Korzybski, *Science and Sanity* (Englewood, NJ, Institute of General Semantics, 4th ed. 1958) 31, 64, 87, 93, 107, 189, 192, 243, 265, 303, 331, 379, 394, 407, 433, 455, 492, 539, 542, 551, 653, 699, 747, 751.

From *Et cetera* 46, no. 4 (Winter 1989) pages 295-297.

General Semantics and Cultural Diversity

by Gregg Hoffmann

B EFORE WE CAN handle problems of pollution, poverty, or disease we must first learn to handle diversity. Unless we can learn to appreciate, or at least tolerate, the differences between cultures and individuals, we stand little chance of confronting the problems that threaten our very existence on earth.

Yesterday, Today, and Tomorrow

Throughout our history, we have reacted too often to diversity with fear and defensive actions. We have felt the need to lash out at people who are different. We ostracize them or even eliminate them.

In today's world, diversity becomes impossible to avoid. Television, computerization and other technological advances bring different cultures of the world to us daily. Commerce is conducted regularly on international levels. The breakup of the Soviet bloc has opened the world to people who were previously denied freedom of travel.

By the year 2000, almost 40% of the U.S. population will be classified as non-Caucasian. We all will face cultural diversity as a fact of life. If we continue to react to differences in bigoted, ethnocentric ways, we will only increase crime, turmoil, and war. We will never unite in the efforts needed to tackle the problems we all face.

I believe several principles of general semantics provide guidelines on how to handle diversity. The principles indicate how our nervous systems, coupled with our use of symbols, primarily language, lead to structuring "reality" in terms of similarities.

Non-Identity

Korzybski, among others, pointed out that no two things in "reality" — from snowflakes to people — are ever identical. He urged recognition of this diversity through the extensional device of indexing: Person 1 is not Person 2.

The principles of non-identification and non-allness can be applied to diversity. The word is not the thing. We can never say everything about anything, or anybody. These principles can be used to make us more aware of our language use — how we talk and react to people of other cultures.

We are Abstractors

Understanding the abstracting process can enable us to understand diversity. Korzybski urged people to explore the territory first, make observations and collect information, and then draw inferences from that experience. He cautioned against that type of higher order abstracting which is not based on adequate exploration of the territory. Among those higher order abstractions lurk stereotypes, ill-conceived assumptions, generalities, and other entities that feed prejudices and hatred of other cultures and individuals who differ from us.

Creating Our Maps

There is a personal element to our abstracting process. Our maps of the world are influenced by limitations of our nervous system, our backgrounds and upbringing, unchallenged cultural norms and many other factors.

We must fight the tendency to believe that our map is the only map, or that our map is the territory itself. If we accept the notion that our map simply differs from another's map — and do not prematurely impose judgments of better or worse — we can learn to listen, and perhaps understand, different viewpoints and ideas.

There are pitfalls in imposing a static linguistic system to an ever-changing world. Dogmatic theories can lead to viewpoints and institutions that resist change. They can lead to "paradigm paralysis." We all need paradigms, but when the boundaries of those paradigms become rigid they can become anachronistic and resistant to new information and ideas.

Cross-Cultural Communication

General semantics also explores our language as a way of structuring the world. We use language to help us make sense of what is happening "out there." We then communicate to each other about the structures we have formulated.

What happens when the languages we use differ in structure? What happens when one person uses English, with its unique structure, to communicate with another person who speaks Japanese, or Arabic? If we do not understand the other language, or are not at least aware of the differences in structure, we can leave ourselves open to misunderstandings. The consequences can be severe, especially when the misunderstandings occur in diplomatic relations or international business.

Appreciating Differences

We can also apply mathematical principles to the understanding of the abstracting process. Milton Dawes of Montreal, Canada has developed a way of using differential calculus as a model to help us differentiate between individuals and cultures — noticing, understanding, and appreciating the differences. Dawes then explores how those differences can be integrated again into a broader culture.

Learning to appreciate and deal with cultural diversity can enrich our lives. It can open up the world to us. It also can make that world a more humane, better place to live.

From *Et cetera* 49, no. 3 (Fall 1992) pages 302-304.

Flags, Symbols and Controversy

by Russell Joyner

In general semantics we try to distinguish between map and territory, between symbol and what is symbolized. Unable to observe, we must infer from their language or behavior when people are making symbolic uses of an object; so we generalize about such matters with some diffidence.

D OES EVERYONE treat the flag as a symbol? What other responses does it stir? Does the flag serve the same purposes in peace as in war? Unanswered, these innocent-appearing questions hamper attempts to think clearly about flag burning and obscure essential elements of this national controversy.

Many Americans have expressed themselves in the press on this divisive issue. Examining some of their letters and columns may prove revealing.

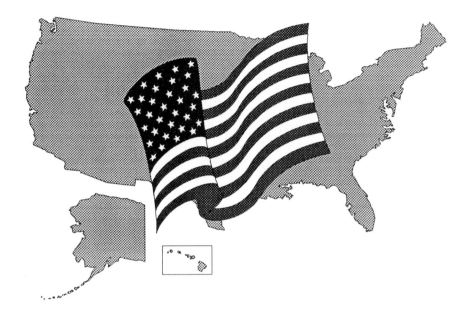

The Flag as a Symbol

When treated as a symbol, the flag shifts attention from itself and stands for something else. To qualify as a symbol the flag *must* call to mind other things. In a letter to a daily newspaper a writer spells out some things the flag symbolizes for him:

> The flag is a symbol. To say that the flag is more than a symbol is double talk. To say that the symbol is more important than the virtue which it glorifies is dangerous double-talk. The flag is a symbol of the freedom that I love; the flag is a symbol for the country that I love, because it values that freedom.... (1)

A newspaper columnist also points out the flag's role as a symbol:

> A flag of the United States is a powerful emotional symbol. But it is a symbol: a piece of blue, white and red cloth....

There are millions of American flags. They are symbols....

Treating cheap flag replicas — some of which are made in Taiwan — as if each were the Shroud of Turin is giving a symbol undue value....

If we elevate a symbol to an exalted status, what is next? Requiring us to bow to plaster casts of the president and members of congress?... (2)

From still another source comes a statement affirming that the flag has a symbolic function:

"Don't mistake the map for the territory." In other words, don't mistake the symbol (flag) for the reality (nation). (3)

The Flag as More Than a Symbol

These writers represent a group that has learned to see the flag as a symbol for other things. There are other people who reject evaluations of the flag as symbol and react quite differently.

Instead of treating it as a symbol standing for other values, they focus much of their attention on the physical object, investing the flag itself with importance. This group responds to the flag primarily as substitute, rather than symbol. For these people the flag *embodies* values to be cherished, even though they may repeatedly call it a symbol. The following quotation, while maintaining that the flag is a symbol, describes how the flag takes on those characteristics it supposedly symbolizes.

...In June 1777 the Continental Congress adopted the stars-and-stripes design as the symbol for the War of Independence. This design carried over when the Constitution was adopted. It was under this symbolic flag that the nation was formed and the mores, hopes, spirit and united consensus of its citizenry forged on a single piece of cloth.

Symbolism is as old as mankind and a time-tested method of emotionally advancing causes. The flag is the symbol which advanced the cause of a United States of America. Had the 13 colonies not rallied 'round the flag there would have been no First Amendment or any others, for it was essentially the principal bond between the 13 colonies.

The First Amendment is clear and concise — no abridging "freedom of speech and the press." If burning the flag now fits the definition of "speech," then the symbol itself must also be "speech." If the flag-burner was in fact "speaking," then he should immediately be tried under treason and sedition laws. The Constitution and the flag for which it stands are too important to the well-being of our citizenry to be destroyed by willful pettifoggery. (4)

For the following writer the flag has acquired unifying power rather than symbolizing that loyalty and unity of purpose already existing in the country. Thus, if the flag is degraded, the unity of the country — even the country itself — is imperiled.

I am appalled at the Supreme Court's 5-to-4 decision allowing the desecration of Old Glory....

How can a widely diverse society cohere in the climate of judicial activism which degrades the power of our nation's single most important unifying symbol? Around what do we now rally to express our love of country? Our trust in one another? Our commitment to uphold our Constitution?

So much for the American history chapter on Betsy Ross. So much for the field trips to the Betsy Ross House in historic Philadelphia. So much for John Philip Sousa and "The Stars and Stripes Forever." So much for "The Star Spangled Banner."

So much for the flag-draped coffins of fallen heroes. So much for the solemn and proper folding of that sacred symbol for reverent presentation to the hero's bereaved family. So much for the proud display of our colors in the Olympics. So much for Iwo Jima, Astronauts on the Moon. So much for the Pledge of Allegiance. So much, I fear, for "the Republic for which it stands." (5)

The Flag as America

The even stronger position of the next writer rejects entirely any role for the flag as a symbol. More than a substitute, the flag is equated with country, liberty and honor — with all that must be preserved; the destruction of the flag means the loss of everything of value, including life itself:

> ...Freedom of speech is not libel, it's not burning the American flag. A man can be destroyed financially, politically, morally, and physically with attacks upon his name and reputation. Slander, ridicule and orchestrated contempt destroy.
>
> We have pledged allegiance to the flag. The flag is our name, our symbol, our honor. The flag is the Republic under God. It is life and liberty. It is the blood of our noble ancestors. It is families and children and purple mountain majesties. It is our past, present and future.
>
> To trample upon our flag is treason. To sanction this desecration is giving aid and comfort to our enemies. To tolerate this treason is death to us and our Republic.
>
> Honorable men and women have sacrificed their lives for the flag. If we don't live for the flag, we seal our own ignoble fate. Long live the Republic. (6)

We have seen that for some people the flag functions as a symbol, as a means of directing attention and concern elsewhere to more important things.

Another group treats the flag more as substitute than symbol. Included in this group are those who maintain that the flag *is* life, liberty, country, equivalent to — if not identical with — what is most precious to protect and fight for.

These two groups assume the leading roles in the national controversy over flag burning: those who treat the flag as a symbol; and people who see and respond to the flag as a substitute.

Historically, some situations argue for reactions to the flag as a substitute, rather than a symbol, for what should be protected.

Among those marching behind the flag in a military parade — especially during wartime, with the survival of the country in doubt — who can imagine permitting a spectator to torch a flag? If such an act didn't disrupt the marchers, they would surely see the flag-burner as an enemy justifying attack.

Understandably, the rhetoric of the flag-as-substitute will have appeal to the many who have learned to associate the flag with our country's wars of survival. To those of us, for example, who will never forget the single-mindedness and unity of purpose motivating the national patriotism and military actions of World War II.

But such unity of purpose and action, we also remember, was associated with curtailment of individual liberties, with some loss of freedom of thought, freedom of speech and freedom of action. Censorship and other wartime regulations restricting freedom were deemed necessary to safeguard information, to combat propaganda, to insure physical security, and to conserve resources — even for a country fighting to preserve individual liberties.

The gradually escalating conflict in Viet Nam, which resulted in very few wartime restrictions, engendered no singleness of purpose comparable to that of World War II. On the contrary, as it continued, fewer and fewer people found reason to support the fighting, more and more opposed it, and the country was torn with increasing divisiveness.

Serving as no rallying point for the nation, the flag was treated with disrespect by a few; and many came to regard it with mixed feelings as the unpopular war continued. The U.S. forces engaged in combat had more to suffer than terrible casualties; they had to endure the loss of confidence and loyalty of their own country, a nation no longer interested in prosecuting the war.

Without a commonly perceived enemy posing a realistic threat to survival, who can we expect to be moved by calls for patriotism? Who will respond with more than lip service (and perhaps legislation) to the rhetoric of the flag-as-substitute?

To review the foregoing quotations of those treating the flag as substitute is to raise more questions: Don't such statements seem more appropriate for a time of national unity inspired by a common enemy? A time when thought is controlled by circumstances of wartime survival? A time when dissent must be discouraged or forbidden?

We live in no such time. Not unity but diversity of thought and purpose characterize our increasingly pluralistic society. While not forgetting our historic wars of survival that produced signal reactions* to the flag as substitute, we now live in a time for increasing, not restricting, freedom of expression: a time for permitting the wide variety of thought and speech forthcoming from a society rich in individual differences.

We live in a time to enjoy freedom of thought. We live in a time for each individual to treat the flag as a symbol for *whatever* it calls to mind and to allow others the same freedom.

If exercising such freedom means that some will occasionally treat with disrespect symbols we have learned to hold dear, so be it.

Freedom is expensive.

NOTE AND REFERENCES

* Editor's note: "Signal reaction," a general semantics term, means a quick, automatic, conditioned, gut-level response to a symbol.

1. Joey Tranchina's letter to the *San Francisco Chronicle*, June 30, 1989 (page A-30).
2. Lloyd Brown's column, Commentary, in *The Florida Times-Union*, June 30, 1989 (page A-25).
3. Alice D. Yarish's letter to the *San Francisco Chronicle*, July 5, 1989 (page A-24).
4. Richard L. Barkley's letter to the *San Francisco Examiner*, June 30, 1989 (page A-28).
5. Tee-Ann Doughty's letter to *The New York Times* (National Edition), July 2, 1989 (page 12).
6. Daniel M. Hansen's letter to the *San Francisco Examiner*, July 18, 1989 (page A-18).

From *Et cetera* 46, no. 3 (Fall 1989) pages 217-220.

How Do You Classify This?

by Robert Wanderer

W E TRY TO DEAL with the infinite variety of the stuff Out There by abstracting and categorizing. Unfortunately, setting up categories doesn't proceed all that easily.

Take, for example, separating manufactured items into "domestic" and "foreign." As Harvard political economist Robert B. Reich points out, "Almost any item weighing more than ten pounds and costing more than $10 is a global composite, combining parts or services from many different nations."

To help the American economy, many companies offer bonuses to their employees for buying an "American" car. But what's an "American" car? Any car made by an American company, even in a factory in another country? Any car built in the United States, even by a foreign firm? Any car, at least half of whose parts are made in the United States? Or perhaps 65%, or 90%? Or any car made in North America?

A bank in Michigan has a "Buy American" plan that doesn't include Honda Accords built in Ohio, but does include Chrysler minivans made in Canada. A company plan in

Connecticut excludes both of these. Most companies, but not all, regard Fords made in Mexico as "not American."

The Monsanto chemical company, which offers its employees $1000 to buy or lease an American car, will accept any vehicle made in the U.S., Canada, or Mexico, since "they use U.S.-made parts and are sold and serviced in the U.S."

Horrors, says the head of the United Auto Workers union in the Arlington, Texas plant that General Motors wants to close — those plants in Canada and Mexico "are taking away our jobs."

The classifications can get quite involved. The Ford Probe is made in America by Mazda at the Mazda plant in Michigan represented by the UAW, but doesn't qualify in some plans. And the Geo Prizm made in California by a joint venture of General Motors and Toyota qualifies in one plan that rejects the Mazda-made Fords, on grounds that GM has partial ownership of the joint facility.

Which is more "American": Chrysler's Eagle Summit made at the Mitsubishi plant in Illinois with 52% U.S. parts, or the Toyota Camry made in Kentucky with 74% U.S. parts?

Further complications: Ford owns 24% of Mazda, GM owns 38% of Isuzu, Chrysler owns 11% of Mitsubishi.

And economist Reich asks: "Which is better, a product involving 100 workers, 80 of whom are in Singapore making $100 a month and 20 of whom are in Tennessee making $500 a week, or a product in which 80 jobs are in the United States paying minimum wages and 20 in Japan involving high-tech research and development and paying very good wages?" He suggests that while the latter provides more American jobs, the former may be better for the American economy as a whole.

Further classification problems are raised by the Customs Service in determining what qualifies for duty-free treatment. At least 50% of the cost of the car must be incurred in the U.S. if payment of duty is to be avoided. The sage Customs Service declared that costs for labor, utilities, and quality control count toward the minimum, but not those for entertainment, travel expenses and factory uniforms.

All in all, a satisfyingly complex example of the problems we face in trying to fit the stuff Out There into the limitations of our categorization systems In Here.

(Source: Associated Press roundup 2-2-92 in the *San Francisco Sunday Examiner and Chronicle*, a *Wall Street Journal* article 1-24-92, and other news items.)

From *Et cetera* 49, no. 3 (Fall 1992) pages 358-359.

"We are faced with the pre-eminent fact that if civilization is to survive, we must cultivate the science of human relationship — the ability of peoples of all kinds to live together and work together in the same world, at peace."

—Franklin D. Roosevelt

On Becoming
an Ex-Centric

by Emory Menefee

I N SAN FRANCISCO, an environmental group expresses its op-position to "corporate greed" by setting fires in front of the stock exchange and trashing a nearby McDonald's. Up the  coast, where environmentalists and loggers are locked in conflict over spotted owls and virgin forests, a group of loggers filed, presumably seri-ously, a petition asking to be declared an endangered species. Violent clashes take place in India between Hindus and Muslims, arising from claims to a piece of land believed by both to be holy. Other violent clashes over real estate occur in the Middle East. In Brazil, the government tries to burn and blast out miners who are destroying rain forests and encroaching on aborigi-nal peoples. Ethnic conflicts in Yugoslavia and the Soviet Union are reported frequently.

Them

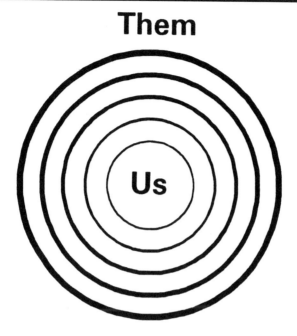

"Our" Cause

All these events, and many others like them, represent a few facets of the urge of many of us humans, either alone or in groups, to push aggressively for "our" cause without caring much about broader consequences or about those who may think otherwise. This tendency, often leading to social conflict, I include under the general labels "centricity" and "centric behavior."

Consider the first example above, involving the notion of greed. Many people believe that personal or corporate greed contributes to many present-day problems. Greed runs up the price of oil when there is no shortage, creates savings-and-loan scandals, allows politicians to be bought, or spawns drug dealers.

Since corporations per se do not think, corporate greed must boil down to a group of decisions made by people personally motivated by greed or other kinds of centricity.

Personal greed appears as a kind of egocentricity that allows us to convince ourselves that it is in our best interests to acquire more of something than anybody else has, be it money, power, buildings, etc. Often the justification takes the form, "If I don't do it, then somebody else will." Egocentricity itself shows up in vast variety, from the person who dominates the conversation (when *we* want to talk) to a maniacal dictator driven by nationalism and hatred. Perhaps the most interesting aspect of egocentric behavior is why it doesn't infect everyone.

For purposes of discussion, the alphabetized list below shows some varieties of centric orientation that readily come to mind. The number could be much larger.

Name	*Some negative results*
Age centricity	Discrimination, rebelliousness, dysfunctional communication
Anthropo-centricity	Abuse of the environment, excessive control over nonhuman life
Cultural centricity	Cultural stratification, snobbism
Egocentricity	Xenophobia, racism, discrimination
National centricity	Superpatriotism, chauvinism, wars
Political centricity	Mudslinging, Watergate, budget crises, civil wars
Religious centricity	Overpopulation, wars, censorship
Sexual centricity	Sex discrimination, homophobia, heterophobia
Status centricity	Snobbism, isolated living enclaves

Each of these examples refers to the behavior of people, not institutions. From one point of view, centric behavior can be seen merely as an extremity of the survival-spawned necessity for people to look out for their own interests and those of whatever compatible group they feel most comfortable in. People have no doubt always grouped together for reasons of protection, cooperation toward common goals, division of labor, etc., all socially desirable and acceptable reasons. The extreme and presumed socially undesirable aspects of centricity seem to involve a "pedestal effect," in which the person or group comes to believe in an aggressive position of superiority, often over another person or group, sometimes over everyone else. Centric opinions tend to overlook the value of solving problems by cooperation.

Centricity and Language

The isolating definitions of centricity usually rely on language, though they may often be supported (sometimes very strongly) by nonverbal props (e.g., boom boxes, "iron curtains," guns). The concept of centricity seems implicit in most of the flawed patterns of thinking and talking that general semantics formulations tell us to avoid: *Elementalism* is a tendency to define and think of things as separate that should be considered as a whole. Centric behavior can be elementalistic because of its claim that an individual or subgroup is superior and therefore independent from a whole society. *Allness* and identification in thinking can be used to define the superiority of a subgroup by remarks such as, "All - - - - are - - - - ," where the blanks can be filled respectively with names and pejorative descriptions of "inferiors." *Two-valued (either/or) thinking* helps to isolate "them" from "us." And, perhaps most important, *lack of consciousness of abstracting* prevents people from seeing themselves and their actions as a hierarchy of labeled abstractions that may wildly conflict with the labels given by others.

Korzybski, Wendell Johnson, and other early general semanticists associated many adult problems with what they termed "infantilism," since human ontogeny goes through stages that are at least partly outgrown by some people but not by others. A child's world may be almost entirely self-centered, with only gradual expansion to include more people as part of a mutually sharing group. Centric people appear to cling to the earlier stages, exhibiting attitudes that can infect an entire population.

Language seems to be the most important weapon in centric definition, and it is often used to justify outrageous behavior. Of course, centric behavior is not always overtly outrageous, at least when curbed by social pressure, but it may still be marked by boundary-setting language, which can be a source of irritation to others. Learning to recognize and circumvent any kind of behavior-modifying language requires practice, and the recognition of centric language is no exception. The following very preliminary list identifies some centric language clues that I have found useful:

- Invoking rights that are assumed to have been invested by an uncertain but "higher" authority

- Sanctimonious denunciation of opponents, while attributing almost invariable correctness to oneself

- Relying on "usage" or "common practice" rather than the accepted law to deny or restrict rights of others, or to justify one's own behavior

- Using some form of power to overwhelm an opponent

- Appropriating or justifying benefits to oneself as "being done by everybody else," "just a drop in the bucket," etc.

- Exhibiting an extreme sensitivity to perceived "slurs" to one's group, while freely abusing others

The line between what we consider socially unacceptable centric behavior, and that which should be ignored or even embraced, is bound to be somewhat subjective, and is probably drawn only by usage and agreement. For example, some of the criteria in the above list might apply to football fans supporting different teams; such support, if not violent, would not be considered centric in the sense of this article. From my own experience, I have found that after becoming "tuned in" to centricity as an abstraction, I not only can recognize it more and more easily but also can differentiate socially destructive forms from those that seem "harmless."

Teaching centric recognition should be easy enough, because examples abound in our everyday encounters and in the media.

From *Et cetera* 47, no. 4 (Winter 1990-1991) pages 393-396.

Abstracting in the News-Making Process

by Gregg Hoffmann

DURING 20 YEARS as a journalist, and seven years of teaching reporting courses, I have become increasingly aware of the abstracting process in the development of a news story.

Journalists are the professional map-makers of our society. They are charged with trying to make their maps as accurate and as close to the territory as possible. It is not an easy task.

In recent years, I have used general semantics principles to help my journalism students at the University of Wisconsin-Milwaukee become more aware of abstracting. I have also tried to use those principles in the field to make me a better map-maker.

Abstracting

We usually start each semester talking about the influences inherent in the news business that affect abstracting. For example, most newspapers try to maintain a 70-30 split between advertising and news; some are at 75-25. The larger figure in both cases reflects the percentage of column inches

devoted to advertising. The smaller figure represents the so-called news hole.

This very factor leads to abstracting, or gatekeeping. Some stories simply do not run because there is not room. There are those in the field and out who suggest that *The New York Times* slogan "All the News That's Fit to Print" might be changed to "All the News That Fits."

Time limitations also influence abstracting. For example, I cover the Milwaukee Brewers for a Wisconsin daily newspaper. The average game lasts around three hours, which means a night game is over around 10:45 p.m. My newspaper has an 11:30 deadline. That leaves me little time to do interviews, race back to the press box and write a story, which then must fit into a news hole (often about 15 column inches).

Needless to say, I cannot take time to include everything that happened, or to interview everybody involved in the key plays, etc. In fact, quite often, the players who make my story are the ones who take the quickest showers and are ready to talk.

The abstracting process in news-making also is influenced by the very bureaucracy of the average news organization. Each story might be read by two or three editors, who add their own abstractions, or delete those of the reporter.

Several learned values, considered very important to developing "a nose for news," also become involved in the abstracting process. Some of these values include timeliness (news is new); the use of credible sources; sticking to the "facts" such as who, what, when, where, why, and how; and objectivity. (1)

Objective Reporting?

The concept of objectivity has been at the center of debate in the journalism profession for several years. (2) Does it mean presenting a balanced view, including as many perspectives as possible? Does it mean neutrally collecting data without challenging sources, etc.? Does it mean journalists simply mirror reality?

The Mirror Analogy

I have spent many a night debating the mirror analogy with fellow journalists. It is my own feeling that the mirror analogy does not accurately reflect (no pun intended) the news-making process. We simply cannot reflect all of reality (the territory). We inevitably abstract and create a map of the territory.

In my reporting courses, I use a mirror (taken from my home's bedroom wall) as a property to illustrate what I feel is the fallacy of the mirror analogy. I will walk around the room holding the mirror, which is roughly 18 by 20 inches. I ask students to describe what they see in the mirror.

We then discuss the things that are not included in the mirror image. What about parts of the room that fall outside the parameter of the mirror? What about the classmate in the next chair, whose ear is the only part of his anatomy that is reflected in the mirror?

Could an analogy be drawn with the details, events, issues, etc., which fall outside the parameter of the reporter's perspective? Or the events which simply are not covered because of the lack of reporters, space limitations or a lack of interest?

I then start to slant the mirror, first left and then right. We discuss how the movement of the mirror affects the reflections.

Can we draw an analogy with slants in news coverage, when the reporter becomes involved in the process? I usually introduce the role of the "map-maker on the map" at this point in the discussion.

An Exercise: Preparing a News Story

Another technique that seems to work with my students is to take a single story and trace it through the news-making process. (See diagram at the end of this article.) I give the students the following information:

A 1987 Chevrolet, driven by Jerry Smith, 30, Milwaukee, collides with a 1988 Oldsmobile, driven by Mabel Jones, 61, West Allis, on southbound I-94 in Milwaukee. Smith was uninjured. Jones received fractured ribs. A passenger in Jones' car, Annabel Brown, 77, also of West Allis, received cuts and bruises to her forehead.

The students then write a news story from this information. A typical story might read:

Two West Allis women were injured in a two-car accident on southbound I-94 about 9:30 p.m. yesterday, according to police.

Mabel Jones, 61, the driver of a 1988 Oldsmobile, received fractured ribs. Annabel Brown, 77, a passenger in Jones' car, received cuts and bruises to her forehead. Both are listed in serious condition at Memorial Hospital.

Police said Jones' car was headed south when it collided with a 1987 Chevrolet, driven by Jerry Smith, 30, Milwaukee. Smith was uninjured in the accident. Authorities are still investigating for further details.

We then discuss how such a story might be covered. Often, it will not be directly covered by a reporter. Instead, he or she will learn of the accident when making his or her daily rounds on the police beat. The main source of information will be a police report, prepared by officers who likely obtained their information by talking to the victims or witnesses.

For the purpose of this exercise, I tell the students that they have been sent to cover this accident. When the reporter arrives at the scene, the victims already have been taken to the hospital and clean-up is underway. The reporter hurries into action, questioning some witnesses. The class then discusses how that reporter is relying on the abstractions of those witnesses.

The reporter likely will also go to "credible sources." He or she will talk to police, who might have talked to the same witnesses.

After he or she has completed the work at the scene, the reporter must return to the office and write. He or she is told there is a 5-inch news hole for the story and a half-hour until deadline. The reporter contacts the hospital to get the condition of the victims and does any follow-up information collecting.

He or she then writes the story, making decisions on what to use and what not to use, how to organize the information, how to write the story in a way that will interest readers, etc. The reporter also must be very careful in word choice. For example, to write "Smith's car hit Jones" could imply guilt that has not yet been determined.

About this time, a student or two will chime in, noting how many "levels of abstraction" the story already is removed from the original event itself. I usually tell them that's just the start of abstracting.

Making Maps of Maps

After the reporter writes his or her story, it will go to a copy editor, who will form some abstractions and write a headline. At larger papers, more than one editor might work on the story. Abstractions are being added. Maps are being made of maps.

Of course, when the readers see the story the next morning, they also will abstract. It is very difficult for the journalist to predict what details those readers will find most interesting and important.

At this point in the exercise, I usually add some information. I tell my students that in the hours from the time the newspaper was "put to bed" and the time the readers sit down to read the story, things have changed. Brown has had convulsions and has slipped into critical condition. The police have found pot in Smith's car. These details are not in the story. Therefore, they can't be part of your readers' perception of the accident.

At this time, the students usually start talking among themselves about the layers of abstracting. I then add one final item. Because the reporter was sent to cover the accident, he or she could not cover a housing meeting that was held on the same night. That meeting will not be part of the readers' world view at all. It fell outside the parameter of the mirror.

I have found these techniques to be quite effective in sensitizing students to the abstracting process involved in reporting. I also have discussed these with colleagues in the journalism profession. Many have said they always were aware of the problems in getting at the truth of an event or issue. They felt the abstracting exercises brought a systematic approach toward explaining the map-making of a journalist.

The Sanford I. Berman Research Grant

In fact, it was on the urging of these journalists that I sought a Sanford I. Berman research grant from the International Society for General Semantics in 1989. I hope to use the grant to work with journalists and general semanticists in developing programs on news reporting and news judgment as the profession enters the 21st century.

Some of the questions I hope to explore include:

1. Could a better understanding of the abstracting process and Korzybski's scientific model make journalists better map-makers? (3)
2. Could general semantics principles make journalists even more aware of limitations of our language?
3. Could we use the general semantics principle of *process* to encourage more coverage of developing issues, rather than a reliance on event coverage? (4)
4. Can general semantics principles suggest ways for journalists to stay in touch with their readers?
5. Would an understanding of abstracting help readers better understand the news-making process?

I believe these and other questions are very important for journalism students, journalists and the audience to address. As we approach the 21st century, the news media will become even more important in providing information and images which all of us use to form our world views. I believe we all can benefit from finding ways to use general semantics to better understand the abstracting process in news-making.

Accident Diagram

ACCIDENT → REPORTER/WITNESSES' INTERVIEWS →
REPORTER/POLICE INTERVIEWS → REPORTER SEEKS
ADDITIONAL INFORMATION → REPORTER WRITES
STORY → EDITORS EDIT FOR SPACE, ETC. → EDITOR
ADDS HEADLINE → READER ABSTRACTS WHILE
READING STORY.

REFERENCES

1. G. Tuchman, *Making News: A Study in the Construction of Reality* (New York, Free Press, 1978).
2. J. Carey (ed.), *Media, Myths and Narratives: Television and the Press* (Newbury Park, CA, Sage Publications, 1989).
3. A. Korzybski, *Science and Sanity* (Englewood, NJ, Institute of General Semantics, 4th ed. 1958).
4. M. Morain (ed.), *Bridging Worlds through General Semantics* (San Francisco, CA, International Society for General Semantics, 1984).

From *Et cetera* 46, no. 4 (Winter 1989-1990) pages 324-327.

Racial Stereotyping in the News: Some General Semantics Alternatives *

by Gregg Hoffmann

T HE NEWS MEDIA have the power to be catalysts for positive change in many areas of our culture. Among those areas is racial stereotyping. Instead, the media often perpetuate stereotyping.

Many of the images of African-Americans, Hispanics, Asian-Americans, American Indians, and other "minorities" are shaped by the news media. It is my contention that many of those images are based on stereotypes. A variety of factors promote this perpetuation of stereotypic images. In this work, I hope to explore some of those factors and offer some general semantics alternatives that could help journalists change their role.

---

* This article was adapted from a presentation the author made at an Institute of General Semantics seminar entitled "Us and Them: The General Semantics of Ethnic Prejudice," held at Columbia University on December 1, 1990.

Current Studies

First, I will give some evidence that stereotyping does indeed exist. A recent study in the *Newspaper Research Journal* looked at coverage of minorities — primarily African-Americans — in four major newspapers in the country. I will use the findings for *The New York Times* as an example. (1)

The researchers found that during the 1950s the *Times* devoted 6% of its coverage of minorities to what was termed "stereotypic coverage." This type of coverage was defined as portraying African-Americans in antisocial behavior or as athletes and entertainers. During the 1980s, the *Times* devoted 12% of its coverage to stereotypic coverage.

In the 1950s, the *Times* devoted 29% of its minorities coverage to "everyday life" coverage — African-Americans involved in careers, community functions, etc. In the 1980s, by contrast, 68% was devoted to this type of coverage.

The researchers also found that the *Times* devoted 65% of its minority coverage to civil rights issues in the 1950s, but only 20% in the 1980s.

The conclusion reached by the researchers was that the changes in "everyday life" coverage were a positive move. African-Americans were being portrayed more often as "regular people" doing "regular things." However, the rise in stereotypic coverage was disturbing, as was the drop in civil rights coverage. The image being conveyed was that African-Americans were engaging in more antisocial action while many civil rights problems had been solved. That reported trend in itself was a stereotype.

My own research, conducted under a Sanford I. Berman Research Scholarship, has shown stereotypic coverage in many of the 400 daily newspapers included in the study. African-Americans most often are covered when they engage in crime or are on welfare. Photo coverage also is weighted toward portraying African-Americans as criminals, athletes, or entertainers.

One could argue that this evidence is primarily anecdotal, but these studies are only two of many that indicate stereotyping does exist. Thus, I believe the premise is valid.

Why does stereotyping exist? It would be too easy to call journalists racists; it also would be unfair in many cases. I believe the stereotyping can be attributed to four major factors:

1. The lack of ethnic diversity in most newsrooms.
2. The lack of sensitivity or awareness of cultures different from white, middle-class.
3. The business demands and professional values of the news media.
4. The expectations and biases of the public.

The lack of diversity in newsrooms is well documented. Fifty-four percent of the newsrooms in the United States are all-white. A total of 7.86% of the total newsroom population is African-American or Hispanic; 1.1% is Asian. Less than 5% of newspaper executives are minorities. This is in a country that has an overall minority population approaching 25%. (2)

These statistics come long after the Kerner Commission study that cited a lack of minorities on news staffs. "Twenty years after Kerner, the newspaper industry remains largely segregated, within its pages and its staffs," wrote Les Payne, managing editor for national and international news at *Newsday*. "All Americans should press for change, because it is they who suffer from a narrow, ingrown, sterile press."

It should be noted that while these statistics are for newspapers only, television and radio stations have not done much better. A variety of factors can be blamed for these imbalances, but they cannot be used as an excuse for the fact that an "old boys" network still exists in the news media — and those old boys more often than not are white.

Lack of Sensitivity

In addition to the lack of proportionate numbers of "minorities" on news staffs, I believe many people in newsrooms lack sensitivity or awareness of cultures and individuals who differ from them.

Almost 85% of the young journalists hired today come from journalism schools. I teach at one and believe the education obtained at such schools is essential to produce journalists who can report about our ever-changing and increasingly complex world. However, I also fear that we are creating a middle-class, professional mentality among young journalists that does not include an appreciation for differences and diversity.

Consequently, many journalists don't think about contacting an African-American college professor as an expert source unless the topic of the story is African-Americans. Many journalists don't think to check on how many incidents like the much-publicized Central Park jogger incident happen nightly in Harlem or the Bronx.

Many journalists don't solicit wedding photos from minorities, or run announcements of church dinners and community events. At a recent American Press Institute seminar, such slights were cited as one reason many African-Americans do not find the mainstream news media relevant to their lives. (3)

When we as journalists — I include myself among the "we" because I still am a working journalist — make these insensitive news judgments, we tell members of the minority community that they don't count as much. We also present stereotypic images to the white community.

Finally, many journalists are not sufficiently aware of the incredible power of their words and the images they create. For example, Milwaukee alderman Michael McGee, a subject of a "60 Minutes" report in November 1990, has formed a "militia" to protest what he feels is poor treatment of blacks. The group wears military garb, and McGee has said that violence is inevitable if conditions do not change. However, the group serves primarily as a fund-raiser for black community groups in Milwaukee's inner city.

That primary role has, however, been lost in the stories on McGee. What has been emphasized is his military image and his more inflammatory remarks. That emphasis transmits a stereotype.

Business Demands and Professional Values

I believe that some of the business demands placed on journalists and the professional values that are stressed in the industry play a role in producing stereotyped images. Prime among these values is what I consider a misguided concept of objectivity. The old mindset of a journalist being a mirror of reality is still very prevalent. Under that mindset, journalists are not allowed to interject themselves into a story for fear of bias.

But journalists must make subjective decisions all the time during the news-gathering process. The mirror image is unrealistic and inaccurate, and can lead the journalist into simply becoming a quotation- and data-collector, without critically examining the input he or she is receiving. What happens, then, when that input is stereotypic? In many cases, it is simply passed on to the readers and viewers.

The timeliness value and short deadlines in the daily news business also can lead to the perpetuation of stereotyping. When a journalist has a half-hour to write a story, stereotypes simply can become more convenient. Often the journalist is not given the time to critically examine the image.

Conflict also makes good news copy. Although journalists work with "facts," frequently they must use story-telling devices. Anybody who has taken Creative Writing 101 knows that the protagonist and the antagonist are needed for a good dramatic story. However, when the news media slip into this format, they put forth two-valued, either/or, black/white images that often are stereotypic and oversimplified.

Another major professional value in news-making is the use of credible sources. "Credible" often is translated into official sources — police, elected officials, etc. What happens, though, when the sources communicate in stereotypes? Often their opinions and images are passed on to the public, and because they are in positions of authority their word is taken as the truth.

The news media also often designate spokespersons for groups. Therefore, Michael McGee becomes the credible source for all African-Americans in Milwaukee. Saddam Hussein becomes the spokesman for all people of Iraq. Jesse Jackson becomes the political spokesman for all African-Americans. (4) Yet, can one individual possibly be representative of all members of any group? Not according to the "allness principle" of general semantics.

I also believe the news media fall into an allness trap when they try to define the "mass." I like to call the media's desire to homogenize their audience the "myth of the mass." What is a mass except a collection of individuals, all of whom have different nervous systems, different personal and cultural backgrounds?

Yet, the news media spend a great deal of money surveying audiences to find out what the mass public wants. That might sound very extensional**, and if done correctly can help journalists stay in touch with the public. What often happens, however, is that media messages end up being tailored for the majority of the respondents in a survey. Therefore, people who do not fit into the majority — in regard to political or social opinions or socioeconomic status — often end up being ignored or stereotyped in media coverage.

Another business and professional factor that contributes to stereotyping is the news process itself. A news story is told through sources, who often witnessed but did not participate in an event. A reporter interviews those sources, produces the story, and then passes the product on to a series of editors. A lot of abstracting is going on during what is often referred to as the gatekeeping process. Stereotypes can be added or perpetuated, especially as that story gets further removed from the event itself. In general semantics terms, the map can become considerably removed from the territory. (5)

The Public

Any analysis of stereotyping in the news would be incomplete without a look at the public — the receiving end of the news product. Many studies have found that the public selectively perceives the news. Individuals read and watch stories they are already interested in. They bring their own biases and stereotypes to the material. Many do not understand the news-making process and therefore do not really know what they are receiving when they read the newspaper or watch a newscast. Thus, when stereotyped images are transmitted, many members of the public either agree with them or do not critically consider them. Even if care is taken by the journalist not to stereotype, readers or viewers might bring their own stereotypes to the message.

Consequences

What are the consequences of stereotyping in the news? Marilyn Gist of the University of Washington concludes that stereotyping limits the self-images of many minority youth. "To the extent that it is a common practice to portray African-Americans most frequently in a negative light — criminals, drug addicts, etc. — or as positive examples from a negative context, strong signals are being sent to African-American youth about what they can become," writes Gist. "If a young-ster wishes a more positive path, which models provide data? Again for most minority subgroups, there are extreme-ly few positive role models in the news; for African-Americans, sports and entertainment are the fare. Might this explain the heightened enthusiasm among minority male youth for music and basketball?" (6)

Dr. Benjamin Hooks of the NAACP addressed the stereo-typed images of many minority public officials: "I have the impression that some in the press would have us believe that before blacks assumed control of cities everything ran peace-fully, marvelously, and only heaven could do better. There was no abuse of public trust, no robbery, thievery, thuggery, plundering or pillaging, no crooked contracts, no killing." (7)

USA Today found in a 1990 study that urban African-Americans were detained as suspects in drug arrests in num-bers far exceeding their involvement. Could stereotyped images, perpetuated by the news media, have an effect on the psyches of officers detaining those people? (8)

Extending the argument to world coverage, how often do our images of other cultures and countries come from stereo-typed news coverage? Using the Persian Gulf crisis as an ex-ample, how much of the coverage was two-valued, ethnocentric, and stereotyped? I believe a great deal of the coverage fell into those traps. Much of the early coverage bordered on outright cheerleading for U.S. military involve-ment. Little critical analysis of the extremely complex politi-cal and cultural situation in that area of the world was conveyed through the news media.

General Semantics Alternatives

I believe knowledge of general semantics principles could help journalists avoid stereotypes and even become agents of change. I also believe the members of the media audience could benefit from some knowledge of general semantics.

How? In dozens of ways, but I have listed ten:

1. First and foremost, I believe journalists could increase their awareness of higher-order abstractions, where stereotypes often lurk, and become more conscious of the gap between the map and the territory through the study of general semantics.

2. I believe journalists could become more extensional through studying general semantics. Journalists should be the explorers of our culture and other cultures. They should be out on the streets, talking to people and interpreting events. Surveys, no matter how sophisticated, cannot replace simply getting out in the world.

3. Through indexing, journalists could remind themselves that not all members of any ethnic group are the same. African-American-1 is not African-American-2. Michael McGee or Jesse Jackson are not all African-American public officials.

4. Through "dating," journalists could get more of a feeling for process and could then concentrate less on closure and elementalism. We tend to tell stories piecemeal and break up reality into time segments. If we are in newspaper work, reality is told in 24-hour segments. If we are in television, reality is divided into newscasts at 5:00, 6:00, and 10:00 p.m. Consequently, we have trouble reporting on issues that continue on and on. We don't do a very good job of exploring why racial and ethnic division exists. We simply report it, too often in stereotypes.

5. Using differential calculus principles, as taught by Milton Dawes of Montreal, journalists could learn to differ-

entiate between members of a group. They also could learn to break complex topics into small, understandable parts and then integrate them into a story that provides the so-called big picture.

6. By understanding abstracting, journalists could realize that they produce maps, not the territory. They could avoid allness and identification traps.*** They could learn to communicate more in terms of probability than certainty. Members of the public also could benefit by knowledge of abstracting in their news and in their own thinking processes as well.

7. By becoming more extensional, journalists might become more aware of the needs of their audience. Needs often are not the same as desires. The public needs certain information, reported in a manner as free of stereotypes as possible, to be able to function adequately in the world.

8. Through general semantics, journalists could become more aware of our language and its pitfalls. Journalists could become more aware of multiordinality and relativity of terms among individuals and cultures. More descriptive language and operational definitions could be used in stories.****

9. I believe journalists could reexamine the concept of objectivity through the use of general semantics. Is "objective reporting" simply reflecting back information in an unchallenged manner, with the premises that we can actually capture the territory and that truth exists "out there"? Or is objective reporting trying to produce a map as accurately and as fairly as possible, even if the process calls for some critical analysis and questioning, while also acknowledging that the map will never be the territory and that truths often are best pursued in an interrelationship between what is "out there" and what is inside our nervous systems? I believe objective reporting can be enhanced by simply asking more questions like "How do you know that?" or "What do you

base that on?" I also believe reporting could be improved through better understanding of fact-inference relationships.

10. Lastly, I believe journalists could break out of some old paradigms through the use of general semantics. For several years, the newspaper industry, for one, has been redesigning papers to make them more visually attractive. I find nothing wrong with redesigns, but old wine in a new bottle is not enough. Content also must be made more relevant and less stereotypic.

Concluding Remarks

I acknowledge that I have probably fallen into some stereotyping traps during this article. I have used some identification in my language and have lumped "journalists" into a group, when actually we tend to be a very pluralistic bunch. Let me assure you, in terms often linked to racial prejudice, "some of my best friends are journalists." Again, I still am one myself.

Certainly not all journalists go about their business in the same manner. However, there are certain mindsets, methodologies, and values that become dominant in the news media — as there are in any industry. When those go unchallenged or unquestioned, they can lead to stereotypes and, to be frank, inferior journalism.

I shall conclude by quoting Walter Lippmann, journalist, critic, and author, who wrote: "The subtlest and most pervasive of influences are those which create and maintain the repertory of stereotypes. We are told about the world before we see it. We imagine most things before we experience them. And, those preoccupations, unless education has made us acutely aware, govern deeply the whole process of perception."

The news media bring images and information about the world to millions of people daily. If we simply perpetuate stereotypes of ethnic groups and individuals, we do a disservice to everybody in our audience. The news media have the potential to provide the "education" to make people "acutely aware." And I believe that knowledge of general semantics principles could help.

NOTES AND REFERENCES

** Editor's note: "Extensional" here means that, in the process of gathering information, one searches for facts rather than taking someone's word for the truth about something.

*** Editor's note: "Identification trap" means failure to note the many differences between individuals who were categorized or labeled in the same way. People who have fallen into this trap believe that Black-1 is the same as Black-2; or all women are alike; or all car salespeople are alike, etc.

**** Editor's note: "Operational definition" means defining someone or some thing on the basis of how it operates (what it *does*) and not on the basis of how someone has 1) defined it with words, or 2) declared what it *is*, simply by labeling it. (9)

1. C. Martindale, Coverage of Black Americans in Four Major Newspapers, 1950-1989, *Newspaper Research Journal* 11, no. 3 (Summer 1990), (Association for Education in Journalism and Mass Communication).

2. T. Pease, G. Stempel III, Surviving to the Top: Views of Minority Newspaper Executives, *Newspaper Research Journal* 11, no. 3 (Summer 1990), (Association for Education in Journalism and Mass Communication).

3. Taken from a roundtable discussion of minority coverage held at the American Press Institute Journalism Educators Seminar, in Reston, Virginia, Oct. 12, 1990.

4. Patricia Hastings of the University of Wisconsin-Milwaukee has found, in an extensive study of *Newsweek's* coverage of the Jackson campaign, that Jackson was portrayed as the "black candidate" and not taken seriously as a viable presidential candidate. He was also seen as a stereotype of "black candidates" in general.

5. G. Hoffmann, *Media Maps & Myths: A Book About News Media Literacy* (Whitefish Bay, WI, M&T Communications, 1993) Also available from the International Society for General Semantics.

6. M.E. Gist, Minorities in Media Imagery: A Social Cognitive Perspective on Journalistic Bias, *Newspaper Research Journal* 11, no. 3 (Summer 1990), (Association for Education in Journalism and Mass Communication).

7. Dr. Hooks' remarks were made at an Associated Press Managing Editors forum in Dallas and reported in the article by M.L. Stein, Covering the Black Community, *Editor & Publisher*, Nov. 17, 1990, 16.

8. S.V. Meddis, M. Snider, Drug War Focused on Blacks, *USA Today*, Dec. 20, 1990, 1-2.

9. A. Rapoport, *Operational Philosophy: The Integration of Knowledge and Action* (New York, Harper & Row, Inc., 1953; reprinted, San Francisco, CA, International Society for General Semantics, 1969).

From *Et cetera* 48, no. 1 (Spring 1991) pages 22-30.

How We Coped with Cancer

by Gregg Hoffmann

M OM HAS CANCER.

Those words ripped through our family in December 1987, piercing our hearts as sharply as any spear.

No disease creates more fear, stress, and panic than what historian James Patterson calls "The Dread Disease" in his book on cancer and modern American culture. The imagery of the disease, historically and even today, transcends its deadliness.

As Patterson writes, "Invested with feral personalities, cancers have been seen as insidious, mysterious, lawless, savage, and above all, relentless."

All those images and others confronted our family when Mom was diagnosed as having sarcoma, a nonepithelial cancer of the connective tissues. Our first inclination was to give up. But we didn't.

Instead, we turned to each other with love and our beliefs in the power of the human mind and spirit to cope with fears

and stress. General semantics principles played a big part in that coping process.

What follows is not THE cure for cancer, or for the stress that the disease causes. What has helped our family might not work for another. General semantics has not made our own fears evaporate, but it has helped make them easier to manage. It has helped make the days since Mom's diagnosis easier to face. I base that on my own semantic reactions and on feedback from Mom and other members of my family.

Shortly after the shock of finding out about Mom's cancer, I started to talk with the family about general semantics, without even labeling it such. Mom started reading books like *Getting Well Again* by Stephanie and O. Carl Simonton, *Love, Medicine & Miracles* by Dr. Bernie Siegel and Norman Vincent Peale's *Positive Imaging*. I soon realized that these works blended nicely with general semantics.

We first tried to become aware of our abstractions and how we could perhaps change our perceptions of cancer. We also became more extensional than intensional. Rather than dwell on the diagnosis and the links between cancer and death, we examined Mom's actual state of being.

She did not seem to be dying any more than any of us are. If we choose to, we could define ourselves, or any human beings, as starting the dying process the minute we are born. Instead, we choose to define ourselves as living. Mom was still very much alive. Therefore, we decided to change the symbols — the words — we used to define her state of being from "dying from cancer" to "living with cancer."

We could not ignore the fact that a tumor was there. However, Mom was indeed living with it. We decided to talk to each other, and to ourselves, in those terms.

Next, we started to actually examine what the tumor looked like. Cancer often prompts abstractions or images of dark, dominant cells, rotting away the body. But the map is not the territory.

Examining the Facts

An extensional look at scans of Mom's tumor showed it to look more like cauliflower, with what was termed low attenuation centers of cancer. The actual percentage of Mom's body that had a malignancy was extremely small. The majority of her body was still very healthy and strong.

We also used an extensional approach to examine what cancer cells actually were like biologically. The Simontons point out that cellular biology tells us that a cancerous cell is a weak and confused cell.

To quote the Simontons: "A cancer begins with a cell that contains incorrect genetic information so that it is unable to perform its intended function. This cell may receive the incorrect information because it has been exposed to harmful substances or chemicals or damaged by other external causes, or simply because in the process of constantly reproducing billions of cells the body will occasionally make an imperfect one. If this cell reproduces other cells with the same incorrect genetic makeup, then a tumor begins to form composed of a mass of these imperfect cells."

This abstraction of a mass of confused, relatively weak, imperfect cells became much easier to psychologically handle than the image of a dark, strong, aggressive invader. Instead of automatically making cancer synonymous with death, we started to look at the disease as one that "may or may not be fatal."

The Whole Patient

We also considered the Simontons' Mind/Body Model, with the addition of some general semantics principles. Korzybski urged physicians of his day to treat the whole patient rather than look at the mind and body as being separate entities. We blended that with the Simontons' model.

Under the Mind/Body Model:

Psychological Stress → Depression and Despair → Limbic System → Hypothalamic Activity → Pituitary and Immune System Activity → Suppression of Immune Activity → Increase in abnormal cells.

If the stress can be controlled, the
Simontons' model is changed to:

Change in Perception → Hope and Anticipation → Limbic System → Hypothalamic Activity → Pituitary and Immune System → Increase in Immune Activity → Decrease in abnormal cells.

In summary, the model contends that a control of stress could lead to biological changes in one's system that actually could help the immune system fight the cancer. It sounded to me a lot like Korzybski's contention that the belief has an effect on the believer, the image has an effect on the imager, or the label has an effect on the labeler. It also sounded to all of us like it was worth a try.

Indexing: Doctor-1 Is Not Doctor-2

Indexing became an important technique. We found out early that Doctor-1 is not Doctor-2. The doctors who diagnosed the cancer said chemotherapy was virtually ineffective and that Mom's sarcoma was one of the fastest growing forms of cancer. When Mom entered the University of Wisconsin-Madison Oncology Clinic, Dr. Ernest Borden, while giving us no guarantees, said the sarcoma historically had responded to chemo at times. We went from despair to having some hope. Stress levels went down.

We learned that Patient-1 is not Patient-2. Each is an individual who responds to the disease and the treatment differently. Therefore, do not automatically assume that you will have certain reactions because others have.

Finally, we learned that Cancer-1 is not Cancer-2. We use the word cancer as an umbrella for what actually are more than 100 diseases.

Dating: Mom-yesterday Is Not Mom-today

Dating also became important. Mom on Tuesdays is not Mom on Wednesday. Mom at 8:30 a.m. is not Mom at noon. Dating made it easier for me and my family members to understand some of the mood swings Mom would experience during treatment. I believe it also helped her understand some of the changes going on within her body because of the chemotherapy.

Mom used visualization and imaging, today's buzz words for Korzybski's abstracting, to help with side effects from the chemo. She looked at the fluid entering her body as nectar, which might help her body fight the cancer. She also envisioned soldiers chipping away at the tumor.

Siegel wrote about a woman who would go to her chemo treatments with a rose in a bucket. She felt she could never vomit on such a beautiful flower. Before Mom's first chemo treatment, my wife and I sent her a dozen roses with a note that read, "To soothe your soul and your tummy." Mom got nauseous but never vomited. The roses? Maybe. Maybe not.

Korzybski's differential calculus, as interpreted by Milton Dawes of Montreal, also became important. Instead of looking at the awesome task of fighting cancer, or speculating about the future, we decided to break time into small parts — months, weeks, days, hours, moments. As a family, we tried to live each moment to its fullest, as if it might by our last. As Mom said, "I feel I'm getting three days out of every one."

I do not mean to paint too rosy a picture, full of false hope and delusion. We have struggled with our emotions, and at times the stress has won a battle. But we have regrouped each time. As I write this, we still have no guarantees on how many more months, weeks, days, hours, moments Mom will have.

Then again, none of us have any guarantees. As I write this, I do know we as a family are coping with cancer much better than we did in the early days of Mom's diagnosis.

As I write this, Mom is living with cancer rather than dying from it. And, general semantics has helped.

From *Et cetera* 45, no. 4 (Winter 1988) pages 325-328.

Management of Stress

by Milton Dawes

G ENERAL SEMANTICS is a discipline that deals with (among other things) the reciprocal interrelationships between language processes ... culture ... thinking ... feeling ... values ... beliefs ... knowledge ... perception ... behavior ... etc. The way we talk affects the way we think; the way we think affects the way we feel and also the things we say; the way we feel determines the things we do and the way we behave; the way we listen, what we hear; the way we look, what we see. The way we look, listen, hear, see, feel, determines what we know and what we believe. What we know and believe determines how we talk, the things we notice, the things we value, fear, want, do, expect, understand, and so on.

Managing Ourselves

In short, general semantics addresses the dynamics and structure of our intrapersonal, interpersonal, and inter-environmental communications, interactions, interrelationships, and as such is relevant to the understanding, orienta-

tion, and effective management of ourselves-in-our-semantic-environments.

Three formulations of general semantics that have specific significance in the management of stress are the following:

1. The map is not the territory.
2. The map does not represent all aspects of the territory.
3. The map reflects the map-maker's point of view.

Regarding Formulations 1 and 2: If we are not aware that we make "maps," and that these "maps" — our opinions, feelings, beliefs, perceptions, judgments, decisions, expectations, hopes, fears, conclusions, criticisms, values — are not identical with our environments, then our day-to-day interactions, communications, and activities will be, to a great degree, inappropriate, ineffective, and often self-defeating. In many instances, the experience we label as "stress," and the psychophysiological damage that results, is a sure sign of this mis-management and disharmony with our environment.

Regarding Formulation 3: Since every individual travels along unique space-time paths, literally perceiving things from a different space-time point of view, we can expect that no two persons will, or can, make the same "map" in the same way. Each "map" will be a unique psycho-biological representation of the educational-cultural-linguistic-social-familial-experiential-economic territories passed through by a particular individual.

Managing Stress

Managing stress is synonymous with intelligent behavior — behavior that is dynamically and structurally appropriate for a particular situation, at a particular time — behavior that expresses organismic efficiency in anticipating, recognizing, formulating, coordinating, and cooperating with asymmetric structural relationships. In other words, behavior that re-flects a high degree of map-making accuracy and organismic conditionality and flexibility.

Managing stress requires constant learning and unlearn-ing, modifying our behavior in the light of experience, re-viewing and updating our cognitive and behavioral "maps" and "mappings."

Managing stress requires knowledge and appreciation of *homeostasis* — the process by which a system or organism minimizes for its internal environment the potential effects of changes in the external environment, a tendency to resist change.

Effective stress management requires timely interruption of automatic homeostatic processes by reevaluating, updat-ing, and even abandoning old "maps."

New Ways

If we accept and remember that "the map is not the territo-ry," we may be more inclined to open our homeostatic boundaries to accommodate new information, and may find it easier to perceive old information in new ways. We may be more open to new ways of "looking" at, thinking about, and doing things. We may be more ready to reevaluate habitual, ineffective, and problem-creating responses, and in this way develop skills in minimizing or avoiding stress.

In a world of infinite numbers of characteristics, the appreciation of others' "maps" and "mappings" can bring tremendous benefits. The more "maps" we study the greater will be our knowledge of the territory, and the more skills we will develop in our own map-making abilities. This will increase our organismic efficiency in negotiating the territory — and *better negotiating* for results with less stress.

NOTE

Editor's note: On page 218, "asymmetric structural relationships" refers to relations between factors that are not equal in importance, size, time of occurrence, etc. For example, if someone has a fever, this symptom is not as important as the underlying cause(s) of the fever. Being aware of this is a requirement for making a good map of the patient's illness. The doctor's priority is to treat the cause(s), not the symptom.

Asymmetric relations establish an *order:* A is more important than B; X occurs before Y; etc. Such relations are not reversible; for example, if E is larger than F, then F is not larger than E. (See "Relations, asymmetrical" in the index of *Science and Sanity.*)

From *Et cetera* 47, no. 2 (Summer 1990) pages 193-194.

How Could I Be Wrong About Her?

by Gregory Sawin

"Yep, she's coming on to me; she's hot for my body. Why else would she be so friendly?" Sometimes, men tend to mistake women's friendliness for seduction. (1) Several years ago, I made this "friendliness/seduction" mistake when I was with a lady who was a close friend of mine. She kissed me

smack-dab on the lips and said "I missed you," referring to my recent one-week absence. I couldn't believe it! I was very fond of her and at last, I thought, she was showing some romantic interest in me. Later, we talked about that kiss and she made it clear that she valued me as a friend but didn't mean to convey that she wanted a relationship with me. Rats!

Erotic Miscommunication

A possible explanation for such a misevaluation is that men have been socialized in ways that lead them to see man-

woman interactions in sexual terms. (2) Kanin put it this way: "The typical male enters into heterosexual interaction as an eager recipient of any subtle signs of sexual receptivity broadcasted by his female companion. In some instances, however, these signs are innocently emitted by a female naive in erotic communication. He perceives erotic encouragement, eagerly solicits further erotic concessions, encounters rebuff, and experiences bewilderment." (3)

Once a man acquires this sexualized way of looking at a woman's behavior, he may see what he wants to see in her friendly but ambiguous behavior toward him. Events that fit our expectations and desires have more impact on us than those that do not fit. (4) A study by Hendrick tends to support this explanation and links the friendliness/seduction mistake to "date rape." (5) However, some girls grow up learning to flirt and play "hard to get," and this may contribute to the problem of date rape. Several studies indicate that sexual misunderstandings could occur when men misinterpret women's nonverbal cues. (6-8) Many authors have maintained that our cultural beliefs about dating could lead to misreading verbal and nonverbal cues, sometimes resulting in rape. (9-14) Kanin and Parcell found that 51% of 292 female undergraduates reported experiences of sexual aggression on a date within the last year. Of these, 24% involved forced intercourse. (15) To summarize, it seems that as a result of social influences in childhood, some men believe that a woman means "yes" when she says "no," and that some women say "no" when they mean "yes."

In general semantics terms, the friendliness/seduction mistake could be described as a man creating a mental map that did not match the territory of the man-woman interaction — he saw seduction where there was only friendliness. But how do people acquire their mental maps? What factors might influence this process?

Where Do Our Mental Maps Come From?

Related to the map-territory idea, Kenneth Boulding wrote, "From the moment of birth if not before, there is a constant stream of messages entering the organism from the senses.... As the child grows his image [mental map] of the world expands.... Every time a message reaches him his image is likely to be changed in some degree by it, and as his image is changed his behavior patterns will be changed likewise." (16) Each of us was born into a culture of beliefs, customs, and a language that shaped our mental maps — our ways of making sense of the happenings around us. These "cultural maps" were prefabricated for us; parents and teachers encouraged us to adopt these maps that told us how to speak, how to behave, and what to believe. As we got older and learned more, we modified some old maps, threw away others, and created new ones. In addition to our cultural maps, each of us acquired a unique collection of "personal maps" values, attitudes, opinions, expectations, and goals. These maps were shaped by parents and by others who were close to us.

Our Maps: The Link Between Ourselves and Our Territories

The map-territory idea is a powerful analogy that is useful for making sense of many situations. The general semanticist Milton Dawes, and others, have explored some implications of the map-territory analogy to help us understand how we evaluate the world around us. (17-22)

Even when aware of our map-making processes, we will still misevaluate some situations, but we should be less likely to decide hastily and be more likely to think of several possible explanations for someone's behavior before drawing conclusions. Our mental maps are crucial links between us and our ever-changing, ever-challenging environments. By being aware of how we acquired our maps, plus striving to make our maps more accurate, we can improve our methods for coping with life.

REFERENCES

1. A. Abbey, Sex Differences in Attributions for Friendly Behavior: Do Males Misperceive Females' Friendliness? *Journal of Personality and Social Psychology*, Vol. 42 (1982) 830-838.
2. G.L. Zellman, P.B. Johnson, R. Giarusso, J.D. Goodchilds, Adolescent Expectations for Dating Relationships: Consensus and Conflict Between the Sexes. Paper presented at the meeting of the American Psychological Association, New York, 1979.
3. E.J. Kanin, Selected Dyadic Aspects of Male Sex Aggression, *Journal of Sex Research*, Vol. 5 (1969) 18-19.

4. H. Marcus, Self-schemata and Processing Information About the Self, *Journal of Personality and Social Psychology*, Vol. 35 (1977) 63-78.

5. C.A. Hendrick, Person Perception and Rape: An Experimental Approach. Unpublished grant proposal, Kent State University, 1976.

6. R. Buck, R.E. Miller, W.F. Caul, Sex, Personality, and Physiological Variables in the Communication of Affect Via Facial Expression, *Journal of Personality and Social Psychology*, Vol. 30 (1974) 587-596.

7. J.A. Hall, Gender Effects in Decoding Nonverbal Cues, *Psychological Bulletin*, Vol. 85 (1978) 845-857.

8. R. Rosenthal, J.A. Hall, M.R. DiMatteo, P.L. Rogers, D. Archer, *Sensitivity to Nonverbal Communication: The PONS Test*, Johns Hopkins University Press, Baltimore, 1979.

9. J. Bernard, *The Sex Game* (L. Frewen, London, 1969).

10. L. Brodyaga, M. Gates, S. Singer, M. Tucker, R. White, *Rape and Its Victims: A Report for Citizens, Health Facilities, and Criminal Justice Agencies* [National Institute of Law Enforcement and Criminal Justice, Law Enforcement Assistance Administration, U.S. Dept. of Justice], (Washington D.C., U.S. Government Printing Office, 1975).

11. A. Medea, K. Thompson, *Against Rape* (New York, Farrar, Straus & Giroux, 1974).

12. D.E.H. Russell, *The Politics of Rape* (New York, Stein & Day, 1975).

13. K. Weis, S.S. Borges, Victimology and Rape: The Case of the Legitimate Victim, *Issues in Criminology*, Vol. 8 (1973) 71-115.

14. J.D. Goodchilds, Non-stranger Rape: The Role of Sexual Socialization. Unpublished grant proposal, University of California, Los Angeles, 1977.

15. E.J. Kanin, S.R. Parcell, Sexual Aggression: A Second Look at the Offended Female, *Archives of Sexual Behavior*, Vol. 6 (1977) 67-76.

16. K.E. Boulding, *The Image: Knowledge in Life and Society* (Ann Arbor Paperbacks/The University of Michigan Press, 10th printing 1975), 6-7.

17. M. Dawes, Our Maps and Ourselves, *General Semantics Bulletin* (Englewood, NJ, Institute of General Semantics) No. 53 (1986-1987) 75-83.

18. S.I. Hayakawa, *Language in Thought and Action* (New York, Harcourt Brace Jovanovich Inc., 4th ed. 1978) 25-28, 91-93, 98-99, 179, 269, 274, 285, 293.

19. A. Korzybski, *Science and Sanity: An Introduction to Non-Aristotelian Systems and General Semantics* (Englewood, NJ, Institute of General Semantics, 4th ed. 1958) 58.

20. G. Bateson, *Steps to an Ecology of Mind* (New York, Ballantine Books, 13th printing 1985) 180-185, 402, 449-458.

21. A. Rapoport, Verbal Maps and Global Politics, *Et cetera* 37, no. 4 (Winter 1980) 297-313.

22. J.S. Bois, *The Art of Awareness: A Textbook on General Semantics and Epistemics* (Dubuque, IA, Wm. C. Brown Publishers, 3rd ed. 1982) 83-84, 184-185.

From *Et cetera* 46, no. 4 (Winter 1989) pages 375-377.

Today's Time-Binders Shaping Tomorrow

by Gregory Sawin

"You recognize that you are one link on the long chain of generations.... You can hear the echoes of history and the generations that walked before you..."

— DAVID M. FETTERMAN

T HE SAGA of the human race has been the struggle to survive, as individuals and as cultures. Our ancient ances-

Drawing by E. Harper Johnson

tors' spears, bear skins, and fire were not their only tools for staying alive. They created languages that served as essential tools for communicating, thinking, cooperating, and solving problems. These language-oriented survival skills proved just as important as the skills for making stone tools.

Universally, on different continents in the distant past, our ancestors created and developed unique languages that made them powerful time-binders. Older generations passed on to younger generations the survival skills, beliefs, customs, and technical know-how necessary for maintaining and improving their ways of life.

As one of today's time-binders, you live in the present and learn about the past for the sake of your future. I believe that your best destiny is to become a skillful time-binder who eagerly —

- listens
- learns
- discovers
- reads
- reasons
- communicates
- writes
- explores

Then you will have the power to contribute your own expertise and efforts to the ever-increasing collective wisdom and accomplishments of the human race in the quest to build a brighter future.

I expect that the present rising tide of time-binding benefits will become a tidal wave of human potential realized if more people in our global community will apply the methods of general semantics — especially the young time-binders in junior high school, high school, and college.

Use the tools of general semantics to tune up your life. Train yourself in awareness of the abstracting processes involved in perceiving, thinking, communicating, and time-binding.

Join the planetary team of time-binders who are working to solve problems and create a better world for humanity today and for generations in the future.

REFERENCE

D. M. Fetterman (Professor of Education, Director MA Policy Analysis, Stanford University), "Hevrah: Our Intellectual Community," Council on Anthropology and Education 1992 Presidential Address, *Anthropology and Education Quarterly*, Vol. 23, No. 4 (1992) 271.

Don't Jump to Conclusions

It appears to me that many people jump to conclusions — they use a mindless, "snap judgment" reflex as their main tool for navigating in daily life. I believe that such impulsive thinking often results in jumping to wrong or premature conclusions based on very little evidence (as shown in the right half of each of the following figures). Such faulty conclusions can result in behavior that is ineffective, counterproductive, or dangerous.

However, to avoid snap judgments, one can learn and practice some basics of general semantics: 1) distinguish between the levels of sensing, describing, guessing, and judging; and 2) become aware of shifting from one level to another.

I expect that rewards for such efforts would include more frequently coming to the correct conclusion, or at least imagining other possibilities in a given situation (as shown in the left half of each figure). This general semantics approach to rational thinking can result in behavior that is more effective and successful.

—GS

Nancy Gaunce's suggestion inspired the creation of this appendix.

Conclusion:
I don't know whether he is a reckless driver.

Conclusion:

He must be a reckless driver.

Guess # 2:
But maybe he bought the car second-hand after it was damaged.

Jump to Conclusion

Guess # 1:

He must be a reckless driver.

Description:

Frank's car door is smashed in.

Description:

Frank's car door is smashed in.

Conclusion:

But they may not be married at all.

Conclusion:

They must be married to each other.

Guess # 2:

They must be married to each other.

Jump to Conclusion

Guess # 1:

They must be married.

Description:

That man and woman are wearing wedding rings.

Description:

That man and woman are wearing wedding rings.

*"Jumping to conclusions
seldom leads to happy landings."*

— S. Siporin

General Semantics Tools

By the use of a few simple devices, called *extensional devices*, the structure of language could be modified in such a way as to take into account process, duration of time, uniqueness, specificity, generality, environmental factors, holistic principles, etc.

INDEXES. The use of a numerical subscript, showing the uniqueness of every person or event, indicating differences as well as similarities, as in: car_1, car_2, car_3, etc., $child_1$, $child_2$, $child_3$, etc., communication medium 1,2,3,n... (radio, television, movie,...)....

DATES. Specifying a date, as a reminder of changes over a period of time. For example, $Communism_{1918}$ as different from $Communism_{1995}$. The indexes and dates are not necessarily written or spoken, but rather are usually used silently, as a part of one's orientation in each situation.

ET CETERA (etc.). To indicate that any statement can *not* cover *all* the characteristics of a situation....This aims to eliminate dogmatic "period-and-stop" attitudes and to develop flexibility and openness.

HYPHENS. The use of hyphens brings to awareness the interconnectedness of the complexities in this world and indicates their inseparability. For example, "space-time," "psycho-somatic," "organism-as-a-whole-in-an-environment."

QUOTES. These serve as reminders that a term is not to be trusted, as it may violate scientific postulates or lead to metaphysical speculations, and that the reader may do well to take this into account in his interpretation. For example, "reality," "truth," etc. Although the use of these devices appears simple and obvious, in practice it has not been found easy for adults, as it requires a change of orientation to a more "extensional" one.

The principle of *non-identity* is at the basis of the system, and is connected with consciousness of abstracting, extensional devices, awareness of differences as well as similarities, etc. This states the denial of any existing identities whatsoever and posits the uniqueness of each individual and each event. "Identity" is used in this context as "absolute sameness in all aspects." Examples of false-to-facts identifications would be: acting on an inferential statement as if it were a factual one, responding to a person as if he were another person he somewhat resembles (father, mother, teacher), disregarding differences. Some identifications may be harmless, some disastrous in their consequences.

....applications [of general semantics] have ranged widely throughout almost every field, in professional or personal life. Far from regarding it as a panacea, those who work in general semantics are aware, as Korzybski was, that results can be expected only to the extent that it is acted upon, not only talked about.

Adapted from "General Semantics" by Charlotte S. Read, in *The Encyclopedia of Library and Information Science*, Vol. 9, 1973, Marcel Dekker, Inc., New York. This excerpt reprinted by courtesy of Marcel Dekker, Inc. and Mrs. Read, who serves as Literary Executrix of the Alfred Korzybski Estate. She is also Emerita Director of the Institute of General Semantics.

Mary Morain suggested this appendix.

Readings and Resources

BOOKS FOR STUDENTS

Junior High School

About Semantics (2-color, illustrated, 16-page booklet that is useful as a supplement to English courses)

Communications: The Transfer of Meaning, Don Fabun (48 pages)

Words and What They Do To You, Catherine Minteer (128 pages)

High School

Dialogue With Street Fighters, Alfred Fleishman (140 pages)

Making Sense: Exploring Semantics and Critical Thinking, Robert R. Potter (245 pages)

High School and College

How to Lessen Misunderstandings, Sanford I. Berman, (30 pages)

Language Habits in Human Affairs, Irving J. Lee (278 pages)

Language in Thought and Action, S. I. Hayakawa and Alan R. Hayakawa (287 pages)

To Be or Not: An E-Prime Anthology, D. David Bourland, Jr. & Paul Dennithorne Johnston, eds. (206 pages)

Understanding and Being Understood, Sanford I. Berman (78 pages)

Why Do We Jump to Conclusions?, Sanford I. Berman (40 pages)

Words, Meanings and People, Sanford I. Berman (102 pages)

College

Bridging Worlds through General Semantics: Selections from Et cetera, Mary Morain, ed. (347 pages)

Enriching Professional Skills through General Semantics: Selections from Et cetera, Mary Morain, ed. (326 pages)

Introductory Lectures on General Semantics, Francis Chisholm (125 pages)

Levels of Knowing and Existence: Studies in General Semantics, Harry L. Weinberg (274 pages)

Manhood of Humanity, Alfred Korzybski explains time-binding. (326 pages)

People in Quandaries: The Semantics of Personal Adjustment, Wendell Johnson (532 pages)

Graduate Students in College

Alfred Korzybski: Collected Writings 1920-1950, M. Kendig, ed. (915 pages)

Graduate Research in General Semantics, compiled by Kenneth G. Johnson (37 pages)

Logic and General Semantics: Writings of Oliver L. Reiser and Others, Sanford I. Berman, ed. (212 pages)

Operational Philosophy, Anatol Rapoport (258 pages)

Science and Sanity, Alfred Korzybski (891 pages)

Selections from Science and Sanity, Alfred Korzybski (306 pages)

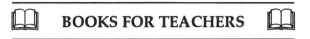

BOOKS FOR TEACHERS

Junior High School

About Semantics (2-color, illustrated, 16-page booklet that is useful as a supplement to English courses)

Words and What They Do To You, Catherine Minteer (128 pages)

High School

Dialogue With Street Fighters, Alfred Fleishman (140 pages)

Making Sense: Exploring Semantics and Critical Thinking, Robert R. Potter (245 pages)

High School and College

Classroom Exercises in General Semantics, Mary Morain, ed. (162 pages)

Language in Thought and Action, S. I. Hayakawa and Alan R. Hayakawa (287 pages)

Teaching General Semantics, Mary Morain, ed. (142 pages)

Thinking Creätically: A Systematic, Interdisciplinary Approach to Creative-Critical Thinking, Kenneth G. Johnson, ed. (325 pages)

To Be or Not: An E-Prime Anthology, D. David Bourland, Jr. & Paul Dennithorne Johnston, eds. (206 pages)

 New Publications

Critical Thinking in an Image World: Alfred Korzybski's Theoretical Principles Extended to Critical Television Evaluation, Geraldine E. Forsberg (220 pages)

Drive Yourself Sane!, Susan Presby Kodish, Ph.D. and Bruce I. Kodish (210 pages)

Mathsemantics: Making Numbers Talk Sense, Edward MacNeal (280 pages)

Media Maps & Myths (news media literacy), Gregg Hoffmann (160 pages)

More E-Prime: To Be or Not II, Paul Dennithorne Johnston, D. David Bourland, Jr., & Jeremy Klein, eds. (368 pages)

Video

Talking Sense. 6 half-hour lectures by Dr. Irving J. Lee.

Computer Software

E-Primer. Interactive computer tutorial on E-Prime for DOS computers. 5¼" or 3½" disk.

Audio Tapes

General Semantics and Effective Communication, Sanford I. Berman (6 one-hour tapes)

How to Think, Communicate and Behave Intelligently: An Introduction to General Semantics, Sanford I. Berman (13 one-hour tapes)

Signal and Symbol Reactions: How to Stop to Think, Sanford I. Berman (1 one-hour tape)

Resources

These and other books, tapes and disks, as well as the quarterly journal *Et cetera* are available from:

International Society for General Semantics
P.O. Box 728
Concord, CA 94522, USA
(510) 798-0311

• • •

Also of interest: "The Index to General Semantics Bulletins Numbers 1-55 (1949-1990)." This index appears in *General Semantics Bulletin: Yearbook of the Institute of General Semantics*, No. 56, 1992. This issue, and most other back issues of the *Bulletin*, can be purchased from the Institute of General Semantics, 163 Engle Street, Englewood, NJ 07631. This index lists hundreds of articles that relate general semantics to other subjects such as art, business, communication, creativity, cybernetics, education, epistemology, family relations, human error, human potential, information systems, journalism, law, linguistics, logic, mass media, mathematics, media ecology, medicine, metalanguages, psychology, social science, and transcultural communication.

Notes About the Authors

Ruth Gonchar Brennan, Ph.D., is Director of Human Resources, BIC Corporation, in Milford, Connecticut.

Milton Dawes, Canadian resident born in Jamaica, is a senior staff member and a Trustee of the Institute of General Semantics. His courses and workshops focus on learning to lead a more productive and fulfilling life. He is the "General Semantics Foundations" Feature Editor for *Et cetera*, and he has published articles in the *General Semantics Bulletin: Yearbook of the Institute of General Semantics*.

James D. French is a member of the Board of Directors of the International Society for General Semantics. He resolved Berry's Paradox (*The Journal of Symbolic Logic*, December 1988), and he re-solved The Barber Paradox (*The Humanist*, May-June 1985). His writings on general semantics have appeared in the *General Semantics Bulletin* and *Et cetera*. French is a computer programmer at the University of California at Berkeley. He earned two bachelor's degrees (English and social science) from California State University at Hayward, where he also studied mathematics and creative writing. He served three tours of duty at Da Nang, Vietnam and left the Air Force as a captain in 1972. He has written and sold comedy material to Joan Rivers and Phyllis Diller, and in the mid-1960s he was a student of the legendary martial arts expert, Bruce Lee. French began studying general semantics at age 17. He was born and raised in the San Francisco Bay Area.

Gregg Hoffmann, a member of the Board of Directors of the International Society for General Semantics and a Trustee of the Institute of General Semantics, is a senior lecturer at the University of Wisconsin-Milwaukee and has been an award-winning journalist for 23 years. He owns and operates M&T Communications, a freelance writing and desktop publishing business. Hoffmann has written extensively on general semantics topics. In 1993 he published *Media Maps & Myths*, his book on media literacy based on general semantics principles. Research for that book began with funds from a Sanford I. Berman General Semantics Research Fellowship awarded to Hoffmann in 1989. He made presentations for the Institute of General Semantics at Roosevelt University, Alverno College, Yale, Columbia, and in Sydney, Australia. He founded the Midwest Society for General Semantics in 1992. He was introduced to general semantics in graduate school through a course offered by Kenneth G. Johnson.

Andrea Johnson, Associate Professor of Communication, teaches general semantics at Alverno College in Milwaukee, Wisconsin. She is the "Education" Feature Editor for *Et cetera*, and has presented seminars for the Institute of General Semantics.

Kenneth G. Johnson earned a bachelor's degree in chemistry, a master's in journalism and a Ph.D. in mass communication from the University of Wisconsin-Madison. He taught for 31 years before retiring as Emeritus Professor of Mass Communication from the University of Wisconsin-Milwaukee. For 30 years he served on the staff of the summer seminar workshops of the Institute of General Semantics, and he is a Trustee of the Institute of General Semantics. Professor Johnson has written several articles on communication, science, and general semantics, and a book, *General Semantics: An Outline Survey*. His credits include the following: Editor, *Thinking Creatically*; Editor, *Research Designs in General Semantics*; Senior Author/Editor of a book of communication activities for groups entitled *Nothing Never Happens*; Compiler, *Graduate Research in General Semantics*; Associate Editor, *General Semantics Bulletin*.

Paul Dennithorne Johnston is Executive Director of the International Society for General Semantics and Managing Editor of *Et cetera*. As part of his general semantics training, he attended the 1989 Institute of General Semantics Introductory and Comprehensive Summer Seminar Workshops at Alverno College in Milwaukee, Wisconsin. He has a bachelor's degree in combined studies (sociology, politics, psychology) from Polytechnic of the City of London, England. Born in the U.S., he grew up in the Bahamas. For many years he also lived in Great Britain, where he worked as a newspaper reporter and editor. He published two mystery novels set in England and the Bahamas, *The Abaco Conspiracy* and *Fugitive in the Bahamas*, and he co-authored two non-fiction books, *Artist on His Island* and *Survive Man, Or Perish*. He also published many short stories and articles. Little theater groups have staged four of his one-act plays.

Russell Joyner, former Executive Director of the International Society for General Semantics (1968-1989) and Editor of *Et cetera* (1986-1989), received the 1990 J. Talbot Winchell Award from the Institute of General Semantics for his two decades of work spreading knowledge of general semantics and its applications. As a marine, he saw combat in World War II and the Korean conflict. In the 1950s, he studied with S.I. Hayakawa at San Francisco State College and was graduated with honors in psychology from the University of California at Berkeley in 1961. He then accepted the position of Executive Secretary of the International Society for General Semantics. As Executive Secretary, he also taught general semantics and coordinated seminars in general semantics featuring some of the country's leading semanticists, psychologists, philosophers, and other educators. For many years he has been an Institute of General Semantics Trustee. Since 1989 he has pursued his long-term interest investigating processes of human evaluation.

E.W. Kellogg III served as Vice President of Publications of the International Society for General Semantics (1990-1994) and currently serves as a Director and Contributing Editor of *Et cetera*. After earning a Ph.D. in biochemistry from Duke University, he held a postdoctoral position at the Membrane Bioenergetics Laboratory at the University of California at Berkeley. Later, he directed the program at the Air Ion Laboratory (U.C. Berkeley) until its dissolution in 1984. He has published more than 30 papers in professional journals on his work in fields as diverse as the biochemistry of aging and the phenomenology of lucid dreaming. He first read Korzybski's *Science and Sanity* in 1976 and came across Dave Bourland's article "A Linguistic Note: Writing in E-Prime" soon after. He has written, spoken and even thought in 99.9% E-Prime for the past 17 years, and has written several articles about the usefulness of E-Prime as a form of general semantics training. Other personal interests include phenomenology, biofeedback and voluntary controls, bioelectricity, parapsychology, and optimal health practices.

Rachel M. Lauer, Ph.D., is Director of the Straus Thinking & Learning Center at Pace University in New York City and Professor of School and Community Psychology at Pace University. Formerly, she was Chief Psychologist of the New York City School System; President of the New York State Psychological Association (School Division); Faculty Member of the New School for Social Research (Human Relations); Trustee of the Institute of General Semantics; Vice President of the New York Chapter of the World Future Society; Adjunct Professor of Psychology, Fordham University and City University of New York, etc. Professor Lauer has received many awards: "Psychologist of the Year" awarded by New York University, New York State Psychological Association Award for "Dedicated and Meritorious Service," Irving J. Lee Award for "Outstanding Research in General Semantics," and, among other honors, she was appointed to the New York State Board of Professional Psychology by the State Board of Regents and the Commissioner of Education.

Ruth McCubbrey, a member of the Board of Directors of the International Society for General Semantics, is a high school English and general semantics teacher in northern California. She developed and teaches a general-semantics-based course, "Critical Thinking," for high school seniors — one of the most popular courses offered at her high school. McCubbrey is a former "Education" Feature Editor for *Et cetera*.

Emory Menefee, current Secretary and former President of the International Society for General Semantics, is currently engaged in research consultation in hair growth and polymer studies, the latter as Adjunct Professor at the University of California, Davis. He is deeply committed to furthering general semantics as a rational and scientifically commensurate model for human interaction. His articles have appeared in *Et cetera*.

Dennis Reuter, an attorney who practices copyright, trademark, and criminal defense law, teaches "Global Thinking: A Paradigm for the 21st Century" (an introductory course emphasizing the overall approach to life given by general semantics) at Yavapai College in Prescott, Arizona. He was introduced to the works of Alfred Korzybski in 1982 while taking a course in practical living skills. Although he majored in philosophy at college and had been a practicing attorney for many years, he was amazed by the expansion of awareness and psychological freedom that resulted from his use of general semantics principles. Following Korzybski's suggestion, he read *Science and Sanity* twice, then a third time. He sought to internalize general semantics, and eventually was successful in integrating the principles with his nervous system to make them an automatic, self-sustaining part of his life. General semantics has been remarkably effective for him, both personally and professionally. Its use greatly improved his relationships, communication skills, and adjustment to change.

Mitsuko Saito-Fukunaga is Emerita Professor of Communication at the International Christian University in Tokyo, Japan. After earning her bachelor of science degree at Tokyo Women's Christian University, she came to America to study. She received a master's degree and a Ph.D. in speech communication at Northwestern University in Evanston, Illinois. Her mentor at Northwestern was Dr. Irving J. Lee, a noted Professor of Public Speaking and an outstanding general semantics teacher and author. Professor Saito-Fukunaga is the first Japanese to earn a Ph.D. in speech communication and is the third female Ph.D. in the history of Japan. Throughout her 36-year career at the International Christian University, she pioneered the development of communication theory in Japan. She is a well-known scholar in the fields of communication and conference interpretation. She is the author of several best-selling books, including: *Science of Spoken Language; Theories of Listening; Intercultural Encounters with Japan, Contact and Conflict;* and *Communicating Across Cultures for What?* She published numerous professional articles in the *General Semantics Bulletin, Et cetera,* and elsewhere. She received several Japanese Ministry of Education Research Grants and Mitsubishi Foundation Research Grants between 1982 and 1990 for her projects. She serves as member of Kyokatosho Kentei Chosa Shingikai of the Japanese Ministry of Education; Chair of the Board of Directors, Japan Communications Institute; member of the Board of Directors, International Society for General Semantics; member of the Editorial Board, *General Semantics Bulletin.* Professor Saito-Fukunaga is exploring conflict resolution and negotiation from the perspective of intercultural communication. She represents Japan every summer when she participates in the Harvard Negotiation Project, which has helped resolve conflicts at the personal, commercial, national, and international levels.

Gregory Sawin serves as Vice President of Publications of the International Society for General Semantics. He is also the "Dynamics of Thought and Behavior" Feature Editor for *Et cetera*; 19 of his articles have appeared in that feature since 1987. Sawin is a medical editor for a pharmaceutical company in northern California. He earned a bachelor's degree in psychology from San Francisco State University. His course work emphasized educational psychology, but also included symbolic logic, statistics, calculus, computer programming, anthropology, archaeology, Japanese, writing, and art. From 1963 to 1980 he studied most of these subjects in his spare time. Since discovering general semantics in 1980, he has read a dozen general semantics classics — beginning with a careful reading of *Science and Sanity* that took five years.

Alvin Toffler is one of the world's best-known scholars on the dynamics of social and cultural change. Alvin and Heidi Toffler have co-authored several books: *War and Anti-War: Survival at the Dawn of the 21st Century; Powershift: Knowledge, Wealth & Violence at the Edge of the 21st Century; The Third Wave; The Adaptive Corporation; Previews & Premises: An Interview with the Author of Future Shock and The Third Wave; The Eco-Spasm Report; Learning for Tomorrow: The Role of the Future in Education* (A.T. ed.); *The Futurists* (A.T. ed.); *Future Shock*; and *The Culture Consumers*. Mr. Toffler has published numerous articles in the *Annals of the American Academy of Political and Social Science* and elsewhere. He has been a visiting professor at Cornell University, a member of the faculty of the New School for Social Research, and Associate Editor of *Fortune* magazine. He has received several honorary doctorates in science, letters, and law.

Robert Wanderer taught general-semantics-based courses in adult schools in the San Francisco Bay Area for 25 years, and has written for *Et cetera* for over 30 years. He was one of the founders of the San Francisco Chapter of the International Society for General Semantics in 1957, and has been Editor of *The Map*, the chapter newsletter, ever since. He studied with Hayakawa, Bois, Rapoport, Murray, Bontrager, and Meyers. He is a member of the ISGS Board of Directors.

Acknowledgments

I thank the members of the Executive Committee of the International Society for General Semantics for approving the publication of this book. I am grateful to the authors and those who allowed me to quote them. I credit the late William H. Schneider (W.H.S.), whose incisive and amusing cartoons grace the pages of this anthology. His clever illustrations have appeared in *Et cetera* since 1954. I appreciate the helpful comments of my reviewers: Nancy L. Gaunce, Russell Joyner, E.W. Kellogg III, Constance Mitchell, Mary S. Morain, Greg and Ellen Phillips, Cynthia Seeley, Kristine A. Thomson, Deborah S. Waxman, Suzanne W. Woo, and my father, Enoch I. Sawin (Emeritus Professor of Education, San Francisco State University). I thank my consultants, Jeremy Klein (Editor-in-Chief of *Et cetera*), and James D. French (an ISGS Director). I especially value the efforts of the multi-talented ISGS Executive Director/Publisher, Paul Dennithorne Johnston, who enthusiastically helped me transform my book idea into a reality.

Gregory Sawin

INDEX

Abbey
  A., 223
Absolutes, 33, 66, 88, 153
Absolutisms, 69
Abstracting, 65, 66, 67, 101, 155, 159, 168, 169, 188, 189, 190, 193, 194, 202, 205, 227
Abstracting
  consciousness of, 98, 101, 154, 158, 159, 185
Abstraction
  levels of, 193
Abstractions, 29, 67, 211, 213
Abstractions
  higher-order, 154, 204
Active voice, 107
Ads, 93, 94
Advertising, 23
Advertising
  television, 27
African-Americans, 196, 197, 198, 199, 200, 201, 203, 204
AIDS, 114, 119
Allen
  Steve, 32, 34
  Woody, 31, 32
Allness, 185, 201
Altruism, 5
American Indians, 196
Analogy, xvii
Archer
  D., 224
Arguments, 28, 31
Aristotelian, 129, 150
Aristotelian logic, 67, 146
Aristotelian system, 62
Aristotle, 153
Aristotle's law of excluded middle, 62
Asian-Americans, 196
Asians, 199
Assume, 18, 19, 28

Assumptions, xvii, 41, 67, 74, 75, 76, 108, 122, 151, 152, 159, 168
Assumptions
  hidden, 140, 142, 143, 144, 145, 151, 152
  structural, 151
Attitudes, 12, 31, 41, 48, 51, 80, 222
Augustine
  Saint, 141

Bachman
  Jane, x
Baker
  M. A., 119
Bandura
  Albert, 27
Barber paradox, 240
Barkley
  Richard L., 177
Bateson
  Gregory, 225
Beck
  P., 123
Behavior modification, 24, 27
Behavior-modifying language, 186
Beliefs, 12, 41, 48, 49, 50, 51, 54, 55, 56, 78, 136, 216, 217, 222, 227
Benoit
  Dominique, 83
Berger
  Kevin T., 21
Berman
  Sanford I., xi, 146, 147, 194, 198, 235, 236, 238, 240
Bernard
  J., 224
Berry's paradox, 240
Bias
  cultural, 64
Biases, 32, 198, 202

NOTES

For more information about general semantics and
ETC: A Review of General Semantics, contact:
INTERNATIONAL SOCIETY FOR GENERAL SEMANTICS
P. O. Box 728, Concord, CA 94522, USA
Tel: (510) 798 0311